7446

D0978204

A Phaidon Theatre Manual
**COSTUME
AND MAKE-UP
MICHAEL HOLT**
111

Series Editor: David Mayer

For D.R.L.

Acknowledgements
The author and the publisher gratefully acknowledge
the help and assistance of the students and staff at the
Royal Academy of Dramatic Art, London for their par-
ticipation in the photographs taken by Michael Prior.

Photographs: Alistair Muir, pp.87, (Oxford Stage
Company production of *Waiting for Godot*), 88-89
(Oxford Stage Company production of the *Cuacasian
Chalk Circle*), 113 (Oxford Stage Company production
of *Tristram Shandy*), Michael Prior pp.15, 17, 23, 24-25,
29, 30, 31, 32-33, 34, 36, 39, 41, 82, 84, 85, 92-93, 96,
98-99, 117, 121, 122, 124-125; Linda Rich p.109.

Illustrations: Jones, Sewell and Associates pp 21,
37, 42-43, 46-47, 48, 49, 50-51, 53, 54-55, 57, 58-59,
60, 61, 62-63, 64, 67, 74-75, 77, 79, 80-81, 90-91, 95,
97, 100-101, 103, 104, 105, 106, 107, 108, 111, 118-
119, 127, 128; Miller, Craig and Cocking pp. 9, 10-11,
12-13, 44, 45.

Phaidon Press Limited
2 Kensington Square
London W8 5EZ

First published 1988
Revised edition 1993
Reprinted 1995

© 1993 Phaidon Press Limited

ISBN 0 7148 2512 3

A CIP catalogue record for this book is available from
the British Library.

Printed in Malaysia .

Contents

INTRODUCTION

Work in the theatre is always undertaken with a future performance in mind, but two artistic facts of life affect this work. One is that no one, no matter how naturally talented and accomplished, can invariably count on inspiration to solve a problem. The other fact is that time is the most precious of all theatrical commodities. The date of a first performance is an unalterable deadline, and that deadline, in turn, determines a whole sequence of earlier deadlines which must be met within the resources, not always ideal, that are available to the theatrical team.

These facts have been our starting-point in devising this series. Inspiration may be rare, but creativity, we suggest, can be supplemented by technique. Effective organization coupled with careful forward-planning can result in impressive productions. Experience has shown that good preparation will actually free the creative imagination and give it room to flourish.

This series has been designed to meet the needs of those working in the non-professional theatre, that is students and undergraduates, school teachers, and members of amateur dramatic and operatic societies. This is not an indication of the standards of the performances to be achieved; some amateur productions are quite outstanding. In fact some of the differences between the amateur and the professional are in the amateurs' favour: amateur groups can often call upon enormous resources for behind-the-scenes labour and the large casts that are so often out of reach of most professional companies. But non-professionals are more likely to be limited by the amount of time, money, space and materials available. We recognize that you will be working with some or all of these advantages and restrictions, and we offer ways of looking at problems which will stimulate the imagination and produce solutions. The answers will then be yours, not ours.

Putting on a play is essentially teamwork, teamwork which depends upon the creativity of administrators and craftsmen, performers, directing staff and stage crews. The team can best thrive when responsibilities are shared and lines of communiciation are always open, direct and cordial. In recognition of these needs we have linked the books by planning charts and repeating themes looked at from different angles in order to emphasize that the best results are always achieved when skills are pooled.

Dozens of performances and hours of discussion lie behind these texts, and while we cannot claim to have covered every eventuality, we are confident that the approach outlined in the following pages will lead to productions that are successful, imaginative, and, above all, enjoyable for you, your colleagues, and your audiences.

David Mayer

Safety

Attention to safety is vitally important when you are putting on any production. When there is a procedure in this book where special care must be taken a safety flash ▲ has been inserted in the margin.

CHAPTER I

COSTUME IN THE THEATRE

THE FUNCTION OF COSTUME

Costume is an essential part of the theatre. When we see a show we enjoy the spectacle of beautifully designed clothes and welcome the stock character costumes of clowns in their baggy trousers and heroes in white cowboy hats. Furthermore we are affected by the more subtle aspects of costume: the psychological use of colour and texture, the careful underlining of plot points.

Sometimes the audience is unaware that the clothes have been carefully chosen by a costume designer. They do not know that the chat show host's outfits are chosen or made to have a particular impact. In the same way, the seemingly everyday or high-fashion clothes of soap opera characters have had the careful consideration of a team of costume specialists. They are drawn, discussed and realized with very specific dramatic effects in mind.

The job of the costume designer is the skilful use and control of all these aspects of theatrical clothing.

COSTUME AND THE ACTORS

Costume is part of the actors' apparatus. It helps them to create their characters. Every item of clothing sends signals of one kind or another to the audience. As soon as the actors appear, even before they speak, the audience will have gleaned a great deal of information. They can see by the shape and colour of the costume whether a character is to be welcomed or feared. The whole image is composed of signs that they will react to both consciously and unconsciously. These signals convey a clear idea of the character's personality. A good costume will reflect the psychological reality of the role. As a costume designer your job is to help the actors convey as much of this as they can.

A costume can also help the actor by being a disguise. Clever design can make a large singer look slimmer, a slight soldier seem well built, or a young man age by twenty years. It can turn him into a recognizable stock character: a harlequin, Svengali or bag-lady.

Alternatively, it can heighten an already well-known personality. The loud comic checks of a Bob Hope film character and the over-voluptuous dresses of Mae West accentuate loved and welcomed trademarks. .

COSTUME AS A PLOT DEVICE

Costume has another dramatic function: it helps tell the story. The clothes immediately show us where the action is set. They place the play in a historical and social context. They can tell us about the progression of a character up or down the social scale as the drama progresses.

Equally, the changing psychology of a character can be described in clothes. A designer can tell us a great deal about the inner man or woman. Sometimes this visual story-telling is as effective as any dialogue the actor may use.

COSTUME AS SPECTACLE

We must not forget the part spectacle plays in drama. It is as essentially dramatic as words are, perhaps more so. Costume can say things that words cannot, and can create effects that a speaker would never equal. There is so much to enjoy in the grand entrance of a royal court, the surprise effect of a good comic costume, the sensuous use of colour in a ballet sequence, the evocation of locale through the texture of the costumes.

THE COSTUME DESIGNER'S ROLE

The heart of the costume designer's job is to use the dramatic possibilities of clothing to enhance the effects the actors are trying to achieve, by describing the personality, social position and psychological development of their characters. To do this you need:

■ a knowledge of costume history
■ a knowledge of costume making
■ an interpretative imagination able to recognize and describe the psychology of character through clothing
■ an artistic eye for colour and shape, and the capacity to describe what you imagine in a drawing or sketch
■ the capacity to work with a team, to communicate well with them, to encourage and to persuade people to do their best work.

DESIGNER AND DIRECTOR

You will be working in co-operation with your director, the guiding influence over the production, whose job is to establish the style and emphasis of the show. A good director will work co-operatively, listening to the opinions of the other creative participants. You will join in the preliminary discussions and arrive at a shared interpretative base for your production. The costume designer's skill is to develop and realize these verbal, intellectual ideas visually.
Working with the director involves establishing a mutual trust. You must be able to exchange ideas freely in discussion and throughout the production process.

DESIGNER AND WORKSHOP

You will be relying on the skills of many people to realize your designs. No matter how small your team is you should aim to use their skills efficiently. All craft workers, amateur or professional – cutters, stitchers, milliners, wigmakers – need clear information to do their best work. You must communicate well with drawings, discussions and explanations. Good craft workers always use their skills creatively, and a wise costume designer listens to suggestions from them.
Above all, give the workshops the right amount of time to do a good job. Help to ensure this by careful and detailed preparatory work.

WORKING WITH OTHER DESIGNERS

Sometimes you will be the only designer on the show, charged with set design as well as costume. But at other times you will be sharing responsibility with a set designer and a lighting designer. In this case co-operation is even more essential and discussion between you is very important for a visually unified production. Make sure you know the answers to questions like these:

■ what style is the director and his design team after?
■ how successful is the set designer in following this through?
■ do we have an agreed colour scheme?
■ do the set ideas call for integrated or constrasting costumes?
■ where is each individual dramatic effect best created – through setting, lighting or costume?
■ do you, in the light of the previous question, need to alter a costume idea to ensure the right dramatic effect?
■ have the other designers recognized the strengths and weaknesses of your designs so that they can co-operate for the best result?

Pre-production Period

Function	Pre-rehearsal Period
Administrator	Check play available for performance. Check score available for performance. Check venue available. Negotiate royalty payments. Pre-production discussions with Director and Designers. Check licensing and permission, especially firearms. Check credit card registration. Gather programme material. Plan publicity. Announce auditions. Determine budget.
Director	Pre-production discussions. Conduct auditions – with choreographer and Musical Director. Announce casting. Announce and initiate rehearsal schedules.
Production Manager/ Technical Director	Pre-production budget meeting with Administration. Design meeting with Director, Designer and Stage Manager. Appoint Stage Manager and technical staff.
Stage Management	Attend design meeting and run auditions. Find a rehearsal space. Prepare prompt copy and provisional lists. Research with designer. Gather rehearsal props, furniture and set.
Scenic Design and Construction	Pre-production discussions. Model making: technical and working. Prepare drawings. Prepare prop drawings. Get Director's approval. Prepare castings and planning.
Lighting	Pre-production discussions. Read and re-read text. Research & Planning costume and scene.
Sound	Pre-production discussions. Read and re-read text. Prepare a selection of provisional tapes. Get Director's approval.
Music	Check availability of scores. Agree rehearsal schedule with Director. Organize a rehearsal pianist. Audition singers. Gather orchestra.
Choreography Fights	Check rehearsal space. Agree rehearsal schedule with Director. Organize rehearsal pianist. Audition dancers.
Costume Design and Construction	Pre-production discussions. Costume research and drawing. Working drawings for wigs/hats/shoes. Fabric sampling. Costing and planning.

Function	Week 6	Week 5	Week 4	Week 3
Administration	Gather programme material. Display publicity material. Open booking if necessary.	Start press stories. Monitor publicity. Monitor bookings. Contact with rehearsals.	Recruit FOH staff if required. Invite critics.	Direct sell.
Director	Attend production meeting. ■ Discussions ■ Script cuts ■ Note running time.	Blocking rehearsal.	Business rehearsals. Rehearsal props introduced. Attend meetings. Listen to sound tape. Lighting meeting	Singers and dancers integrated. Reblocking. ■ Pianist present. Orchestral rehearsal
Production Manager	Costing meetings with set, prop and costume makers. Production meeting. Problem solving and budget decisions.	Coordinating technical departments and budget control.		Progress meeting. Arrange for equipment Liaison with venue.
Stage Management	Mark out and prepare rehearsal space. Note script changes. Attend production and props meetings.	Run rehearsal Prop, furniture and dressings search and making. Liaison with all departments.		Attend progress meetin Arrange sound and light meetings for director
Scenic design and construction	Meetings and planning with technical director. ■ Attend read through Call for actors, staff and workshop. Scenic construction and propmaking.	Liaison with SM and workshop. ■ Buy soft furnishings.	■ Choose hire furniture and scene painting.	Drawings for new prop: Alterations as necessary
Costume design and construction make up	Attend first rehearsal.	Check stock Measure all actors Buy fabrics Order wigs	Preliminary fittings Cutting and making	Keep in touch with rehearsals for new costume ideas Sort shoes
Lighting	Attend production meeting. Keep in contact rehearsals – SM/Director/Designer. Liaison with Director and Designer	Artwork and photography for projection. ■ Construction special lighting affects.	■ Check stock.	Attend rehearsal and ru through.
Sound	Attend production meeting. Basic provisional tape in rehearsal.	Research and planning. ■ Check stock and buy in tapes, effects records, etc. Meeting with director.	Prepare effects tapes. Sound meetings with director.	Record special effects. Record hire effects with actors. ■ Design sound rig. ■ Hire equipment.
Music	Singing rehearsals. Music rehearsals.			Singers join main rehea
Choreography and fights	Dancing rehearsals. Fight rehearsals.		Hire weapons with SM.	Fights choreographed. Dancers join main rehea

Week 2	Day 7	Day 6	Day 5	Day 4	Day 3	Day 2	Day 1
rite press to otocall.	Check Box. Engage FOH staff. ■ Ushers. ■ Sales. ■ Box Office.	Train FOH staff. Arrange FOH displays. Print programmes.				Photo call.	
ish rehearsal. Fights in rehearsal. et to discuss lighting. et with sound dept, to eck final FX.	Introduce performance props.		Run through	Attend lighting and sound plotting sessions.	Attend technical rehearsal and give notes.	Photo call, dress rehearsal give notes.	Final dress rehearsal and gives notes.
ke up production edule. Arrange transport staff for the get in/fit up show staff.	Supervise get in and fit up as per production schedule	Continue fit up as per schedule (+ LX main rig).	Continue as per schedule. Possible fire inspection	Supervise schedule. (LX and sound plotting sessions).	Attend technical rehearsal.	Supervise technical work on stage. Attend dress rehearsal.	Supervise technical work on stage. Attend final dress rehearsal.
range lighting designer to e an early run through. rector to listen to sound e. Prepare setting lists d cue sheets.	Run rehearsals. Team attend run through. Finalize setting lists, cue sheets	Help fit up paint etc. Final props adjustments.	Team help move out of rehearsal rooms to venue.	Dress the set Set the props. Attend LX and sound plotting sessions.	Possible scene change rehearsal. Run technical rehearsal.	Run Dress rehearsal. Attend Director's note session.	Run final dress rehearsal.
op meetings to check all ops. tend Lighting Discussion.	Fit up and painting as per production.	Continue fit up and painting as per production schedule.	Fit up and paint end texture as per schedule.	Attend lighting session and LX plotting. Dress the set.	Attend technical rehearsal.	Attend photo call. Attend dress rehearsal.	Technical work as necessary. Attend dress rehearsal.
cessories found/bought cond or final fittings	Check costumes, Check wigs arrived.	Get in for costumes. Costumes to dressing rooms.	Attend run through.	Attend run through Check make up.	Attend technical rehearsal. Check make up under lights.		
	Finalize copy lighting design. Preliminary rigging. Hired equipment arrives.	Lighting rigging.	Focusing of lighting.	Lighting session plotting.	Technical rehearsal.	Dress rehearsal. Attend notes sessions. Technical work on stage.	Final dress rehearsal. Technical work on stage.
eparation of final tapes. Rehearse live sound xing – mini-tech. rector to hear tape.	Hired equipment arrives. Mini sound tech with orchestra.	Sound rigging.	Attend run through.	Sound plotting rework tapes.	Technical rehearsal. Rework tapes.	Dress rehearsal. Rework tapes. Attend notes session.	Final dress rehearsal. Attend notes session.
sicians rehearse with und reinforcement if cessary.				Rehearsal for orchestra and cast.	Technical rehearsal, piano only.	Dress rehearsal with orchestra.	
hts join main rehearsal.		Choreographer present as needed.					

The Run and Post Production

Function	The Run	Post Production
Administrator	Show reports to Director. FOH staff checks. Monitor sales. Liaise with Stage Manager.	File prompt script and production paperwork. Collect scripts. Pay accounts.
Director	Note running times. Director's notes to cast. Warnings and encouragement before performance. Keep contact with SM for problems.	File director's script. Compile report on production and contact list for cast or production team.
Production Manager	Work on budget accounts with Administration.	Arrange transport and staff for get-out. Supervise get-out and storage of any stock set. Supervise returns of hired/borrowed equipment. Final work on accounts with Administration
Stage Management	Run shows as per prompt script, running lists, etc. Check set, props, furniture settings. Supervise understudy rehearsals. Show reports.	Get out props, dressings and furniture. Supervise return of hired and borrowed items and stock to stores. Assemble prompt script and all lists, plots, etc. for the show and file with Administration.
Scenic Design and Construction		Sort out scenic stock to keep with Production Manager.
Lighting	Check performances crew present. Check equipment pre-performance. Run Show.	Dismantle and store lighting equipment. Return hired equipment. File lighting plot.
Sound	Check performances crew present. Check equipment pre-performance. Run Show.	Dismantle and store sound equipment. Store tapes and catalogue for future. Return hired equipment.
Costume Design		Cleaning and storage of costumes. File costume Bible.

THE TEAM

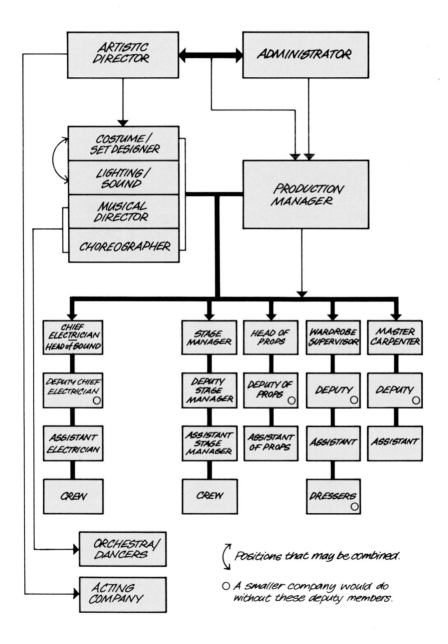

ARTISTIC DIRECTOR ↔ ADMINISTRATOR

COSTUME / SET DESIGNER
LIGHTING / SOUND
MUSICAL DIRECTOR
CHOREOGRAPHER

PRODUCTION MANAGER

CHIEF ELECTRICIAN HEAD of SOUND
DEPUTY CHIEF ELECTRICIAN ○
ASSISTANT ELECTRICIAN
CREW

STAGE MANAGER
DEPUTY STAGE MANAGER
ASSISTANT STAGE MANAGER
CREW

HEAD OF PROPS
DEPUTY OF PROPS ○
ASSISTANT OF PROPS

WARDROBE SUPERVISOR
DEPUTY ○
ASSISTANT
DRESSERS ○

MASTER CARPENTER
DEPUTY ○
ASSISTANT

ORCHESTRA / DANCERS

ACTING COMPANY

⟨ Positions that may be combined.

○ A smaller company would do without these deputy members.

THE COSTUME DESIGNER'S PRODUCTION DIARY

It is impossible to present a universal production diary suited to every type of theatrical circumstance. Use the one given here as an indication of the areas that will fall within your responsibility as costume designer. Always cross-check what the other members of the production team are doing. Communication is very important at all times.

PRE-PRODUCTION PERIOD

This is a time of planning and preparation; for sorting out production approaches and ideas in discussions, preparing drawings, and altering them after further talks.

A great deal will be expected of you. First, you will need to be familiar with the text to enter fully into discussions with the director and other designers. Next, you will be producing proposals in visual form and modifying or altering them as ideas are refined.

It will be necessary to check budgets and make sure they are adequate for the realization of your designs.

Now is the time to assemble a team of people who can actually make the costumes: cutters, stitchers, milliners etc. Also arrange workshop facilities and check the availability of costume and wig hire companies.

The better you use this period for preparation the freer you will be during the making process. Eliminate as many problems here as you can; you will need time later to face a different kind of creative process.

PRODUCTION PERIOD

As costume designer you will be expected to attend the read through in order to present your costume designs to the actors. Put yourself in their place and remember that you will be selling your ideas to them. Point out the advantages of your proposals and indicate any restriction of movement, or special features. It is a good idea to get photocopies of your drawings. Give them to each actor or hang them in the rehearsal room so that they are kept in mind.

During this period establish and maintain lines of communication with the rehearsals. Visit them as often as you can, and make sure that the stage management keep you informed of how costume is to be used and any new costume proposals that may crop up. Always examine these suggestions carefully, making sure that you understand what is asked for and that your solutions are the right ones.

One of your first jobs will be the buying of fabrics and decorative trimmings for the costumes. You will also be following the work in the workshops at this time, attending fittings, visiting hire companies, and dealing with wig hire. Remember that the clearer the information you give, the better the results will be.

FIT-UP DRESS REHEARSALS, OPENING NIGHT

At the fit-up you will be making sure that a suitable workshop is available for the mounting of the production, and that it is fitted for the maintainance of the costumes throughout the play's run.

A costume parade may be necessary if the cast is very large, and you should make provision for it to be held with the director present. But a small-cast play will not need this rather cumbersome event.

At the dress rehearsal you will be busy checking that actors are wearing their costumes correctly, and that they are able to perform all their actions comfortably in them. You should also keep an eye on colour and other design effects to make sure that they work properly or can be made to do so.

On the first night your role is a supportive one giving encouragement to the company and director, and seeing just how far you have been able to anticipate the audience reaction correctly.

Do not forget that in some companies you will be required for the post-production period. The theatre must be cleared of your temporary wardrobe, and costumes must be returned to storage or the hire company.

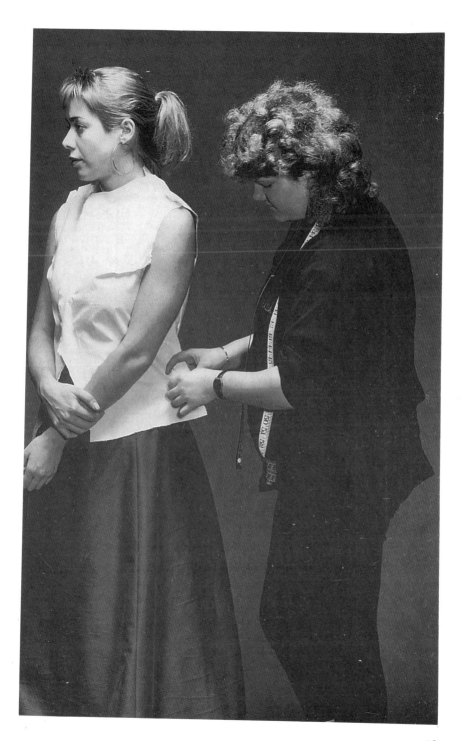

GENRE AND STYLE

Appreciating the chemistry of a play is the essential first step in costume design. If you do not judge this correctly you may work in an inappropriate design style and your costumes may have the wrong effect.

Of course every play contains a number of anomalies. There are comic characters within many tragedies but their context nonetheless demands an adjustment of design style to suit the overall mood of the drama. After your first readings of the play you will be able to judge from the plot structure, and the language and the conventions used, what kind of play you are dealing with. An approach to realizing the text will emerge from discussions with the director. This will enable you to choose a style to work in, such as realism, abstract design, or neo-realism. You will then be well prepared to design each character within the context of your particular chosen style.

UNDERSTANDING THE CHARACTERS

Your next reading of the play must focus on finding out about the individual characters. You are seeking to understand their personalities. Always bear in mind that a good costume reflects the character's personality. Tackle each scene separately and ask yourself some questions:

■ what is the overall mood of the scene?
■ what is the function of the character in this scene – heroine, comic, stooge, decorative?
■ what list of adjectives best describes their character?
■ have they changed personality even slightly from the last scene?
■ what is their relationship to the other characters?
■ how important are they in the scene – are they background or foreground figures?

You are trying to discover two things: the personality of each character and their dramatic function. Your designs will try to reflect their psychology and personality in the shape and colours you use. Adapt what you

Finished costumes in a production result from careful design analysis combined with the chosen production style.

feel they would wear to suit the dramatic function of the character within each scene.

PREPARING A COSTUME PLOT

It is a good idea to prepare a costume plot like the one here . This presents the play in terms of its costumes. It will give you an immediate list of priorities, an early warning of possible problems, and a comprehensive check-list to work from.

How many costumes?

The script will tell you how many costumes you need. Count carefully; you will find extra costumes not indicated directly in the text. Remember that a change of costume can be used to imply a number of things. It can indicate a lapse of time, a change in social position, or a mood change. Costume can be a really effective way of underlining a dramatic point indicated by the playwright.

You will notice in your script various indications of what the costumes should look like, a colour, a fabric, or a texture. These will come from the author's stage directions and also from remarks made by one character about another. You must decide which of these are absolutely necessary and indicate them on the costume plot.

Shoes and wigs

Footwear and hairstyles complete a costume, and require much care. Make sure that your costume plot indicates how many shoes and wigs are required. They are expensive items so count carefully. Your budget will determine what you can have, and it may be necessary to indicate alternative solutions on the list. You can, for instance, use hats to cover heads or use the actors' own hair. One pair of shoes might be chosen in a neutral colour to accompany a number of costume changes. Be prepared to be very inventive in these fields.

Quick changes

Identify any quick changes at this stage. How quick the change will be depends on a number of things – the time allowed in the script, the complexity of the costumes, the position of the actor on stage, and the director's skill in organizing the change period. You should note on the costume plot if you think there is a quick change so that fastenings and other construction points can be conveniently designed.

COSTUME PLOT FO:		
ACT I THE HELME Dec 23rd 1876 5 p.m		
	COSTUME	ACCESSOR
NORA Lawyer's wife	Day dress	Hat Coat Gloves (fo shopping Wig
TORVALD an ambitious lawyer	Lounge suit	
Dr. RANK A Doctor of independent means)	Doctor's Frock-coated suit	Furlined overcoat Pocket watch
Mrs. LINDE Widowed secretary	Suit Blouse	Travelling Cape, Bon. Gloves, Ba Own Hair
NILS KROGSTAD Lawyer	Office Suit with Frock Coat	Overcoat Hat Scarf
NURSE	Nurse's Outfit	Gloves Cape (for walk in s with child Cap
MAID	Maid's outfit	and Cap
CHILD I EMMY (5 years old ?)	Velvet dress	Coat, Ha Gloves Scarf
CHILD II BOB (6 years old?)	Breeches Suit	Coat, Ha Gloves Scarf
CHILD III IVAR (11 years old?)	Breeches Suit	Coat, H Gloves Scarf

DOLLS HOUSE" BY HENRIK IBSEN

RTMENT	ACT II THE SAME Dec 24th 1876 6 pm			ACT III THE SAME Dec 24th 1876 Late night		
OTWEAR	C	A	F	C	A	F
ts for / a outdoor / indoor / ar	Afternoon Dress	Hat Coat (as before) Wig	Same	1 Fancydress Tarantella costume (Fancy Dress) 2 Travelling outfit (skirt blouse, jacket)	1 Shawl for costume 2 Shawl to depart in. Wig	
n shoes	Office suit (dark grey)	Overcoat	Black shoes	Evening Dress	Long Opera cape	Patent Shoes
k shoes	Dark formal suit	Same	Same	Evening Dress	Cape	Patent Shoes
ts	As Act I	As Act I	Same	Better Evening Dress	As Act I	Different Shoes
ck es	Less formal suit (he is out drinking)	Same	Boots	As Act II	As Act II	Boots (Act II)
ts	Same		Same			
ts				Same		Same
ts						
ts						
es						

CHAPTER 2

PREPARING COSTUME DRAWINGS

THE BASIC FIGURE

Your costume drawing is a means of showing details of the costume that you propose for the character. It does not have to be a classic figure drawing, a work of art in itself. But it must be intelligible, so if your drawing skills are weak you should learn how to represent the human figure at least in a very basic way.

As well as the standard front view you may need to show a side or three-quarter view to explain your ideas properly.

It is essential that the costume is presented in feasible proportions. It would be pointless to indicate something which cannot be achieved without an impossible distortion of the actor's body. It will help enormously to be familiar with the proportions of the basic human figure.

You can also express a great deal by the body position of the character in your design. You might try to draw them in such a way as to reflect personality in their stances.

THE FIGURE AS GEOMETRIC CONSTRUCTION

It is helpful to see the human figure as a geometric construction – a series of cylinders, cones, and spheres.

The drawing shown here uses this idea. The head is seen as a sphere on the cylinder of the neck. The chest and the trunk are a coupling of inverted cones, and the arms and legs are jointed cylinders. Of course the basic shapes must be slightly squashed for complete reality, but by thinking of the body in this three-dimensional way you will be able to manipulate the drawing for your purposes.

Consider the costume around the body in the same way. Collars, trousers and sleeves become cylinders fitted around the neck, legs and arms. A skirt is a truncated cone placed over the waist.

Always sketch a centre line down the body, tracing it sculpturally over the sphere of the head, down the cylinder of the neck and across the body. This will help you to position buttons and lapels correctly.

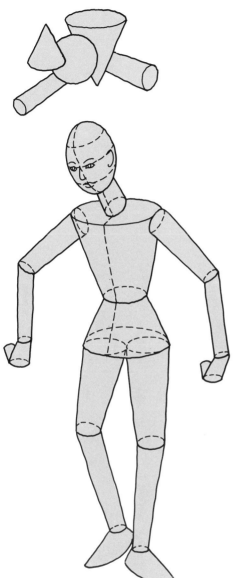

USING A STENCIL

In preparing a series of sketches you may find it useful to make a stencil of a basic figure. You can draw the period outline shape on thin card and cut it out. Drawing round this simple tool enables you to reproduce figures very quickly. You can achieve a variety of stances by turning the stencil over occasionally. Its advantages are:

■ in the preparatory stages you can save time with quick stencil outlines and concentrate on the ideas for the actual costumes
■ a whole chorus can be drawn with small variations of detail and colour on a basic shape
■ you may wish to use the period outlines in this book (see page 44), preparing a stencil from the superimposed grid pattern.

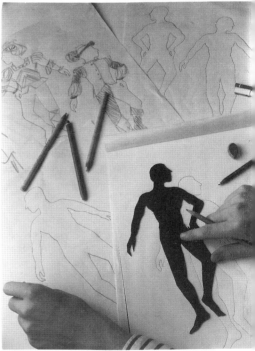

Basic proportions
The head fits seven times into the body.
Arms reach to mid-thigh when extended straight down.
On the face, the eyes are two-thirds of the way up the head. The tops of the ears are level with the eyes, and the nose is within the lower half of the head.

The drawings show the figure as a construction of cones, spheres and cylinders. The collar is a neck cylinder, the hat a head cylinder. Both figure drawings have a coloured centre line.
A stencil is used to produce different drawings, perhaps of a Roman soldier. The card cut-out is turned and moved for multiple figure stances.

CHOOSING A MEDIUM

All costume designers have their own style of costume drawing. You will quickly develop your own, finding a method and medium that you feel comfortable with. But never lose sight of the purpose of a costume sketch.

The designer's artwork is the starting point for further creativity. You will use it for inspiration about fabric choices, the wardrobe supervisor will allocate skills according to the work it suggests, the cutters will be guided by it, and the actor will be bearing it in mind as he or she prepares.

Imaginative contributions will be stimulated by what you communicate and the way in which you express it. You should therefore develop a style and choose a medium which will inspire the kind of invention you are hoping for.

USING 'GIVENS'

You do not have to do your own drawings. If it is very difficult for you, you can use photographs, paintings, costume books or photostats from them to demonstrate what you suggest for a costume. You may prepare a collage of these 'givens' or just present them to your supervisor.

This is a very uninspiring method, offering little interpretive inspiration. It may be useful for absolute historical accuracy but you should be aware that what will be interpreted is the work of the original artist or photographer. You will have to choose your material carefully to ensure that you are in control of character interpretation through it.

USING PAINT

Paint is a very expressive medium and you should learn to use it with a great degree of control. With it you can communicate much about colour, texture and shape. The painting process is itself a means of invention with accidental effects frequently occurring as you work.

There are many techniques to consider using:

Watercolour

This painting process involves the building up of coloured areas with a series of tinted washes. This creates drawings which frequently inspire the use of layers of translucent gauze fabrics on costumes. It is an ideal medium for ballet costumes.

Gouache

This is an ideal costume designer's medium. It can be used like watercolour for translucent impressions or applied thickly in opaque layers for denser effects. It therefore suggests a whole variety of fabric types.

Sprayed effects

You might like to try spraying around your drawing stencil to form a background to your figure sketch, or even to build up a whole drawing with coloured sprays. Use a mouth-spray or even an aerosol car-spray. It is also possible to flick paint from a toothbrush for an interesting effect.

These techniques may inspire the inventive treatment of the surface of your fabrics with paints, glues or other additions.

Line and wash

To indicate what you see as the construction of the costume with great clarity, you may consider using simple line drawings with washes of colour. This method puts a lot of resposibility on to the costume cutters. The simpler the drawing, the more exposed their work will be in its interpretation. Make sure that you have experienced and skilful people for this work.

USING COLLAGE

It is also possible to build up a costume drawing as a collage. You form the sketch by gluing together cut-out pieces of magazine pictures, fabrics, tissue papers etc. You should try to get basic proportions right, but the figure drawing involved in this technique will be rudimentary.

Collage sketches inspire very inventive responses from the wardrobe staff. Interpreting and realizing the accidental effects of the cut-outs may involve altering fabrics completely – dyeing them, putting layers of lace on top, or sticking polystyrene beads all over them. The resulting costumes are frequently highly imaginative and expressive of personality.

TECHNICAL SKETCHES

Since your costume sketch is primarily designed to convey personality and character, it may not always be very detailed. You may need to add technical sketches to indicate specific requirements.

You may be willing to leave the interpretation of construction entirely to the supervisor and cutter. Such a decision will largely depend on the relationship you have with them. You may feel that you can communicate any technical points through discussion. But remember that you can only rely on getting what you specify.

Any interpreter of your ideas will probably need additional information of two kinds:

Points of construction

It can be very helpful if you indicate by a line drawing the kind of period construction you are expecting to be used. The number and placing of seams, the specific pattern or a reference source can all be indicated, if you feel that the cutter may not know what is needed.

Details of underwear and corsetry can be shown through line drawings, photostats or written notes.

Sometimes you will need to explain special effects that must be built into the costume – trick shoulder-pads, concealed lighting devices, or reversible linings.

If the shape of the actor is to be changed with padding, a technical sketch to be given to a specialist maker may be needed.

One of the most helpful extra drawings you can provide is a rear view of the whole costume.

Points of amplification

A technical sketch can explain a detail too blurred or too small to be clear in the costume drawing. With a line drawing and notes about measurements etc., you can specify such things as the size and kind of cuffs required, the shape and decoration of a skirt flounce, or the construction of a cravat.

Do not forget to tell the makers about hidden details such as pocket positions.

Notes can indicate any special requirements you may have about the use of fabrics in juxtaposition or layers.

Take care to show the placing of braids and other trimmings on the costume. It is helpful to give measurements wherever possible.

MEASURING THE ACTORS

No costumes can be made without a comprehensive list of measurements for every actor. These should be taken the moment they arrive, to prevent any delay once the costume making starts. Keep them up to date: an actor's measurements may fluctuate from time to time. Beware of any measurement not verified with a tape measure. People frequently underestimate the shape of their figures!

Follow these diagrams to establish a systematic method of measuring.

Head measurements are particularly important. You will use them for wigs and headwear, both of which need accurate fitting.

Neck measurements and collar sizes are different things. Be sure to take both measurements.

Measure the outside arm length with the elbow bent to ensure a sleeve that is long enough.

The measurement across the back is particularly important; a chest size may not guarantee that a jacket fits properly.

Take care to locate the waist very carefully. It is sometimes elusive.

You need both inside and outside leg measurements on a man. Waist to ground is essential for the correct skirt length on a woman.

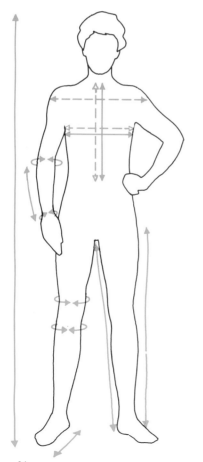 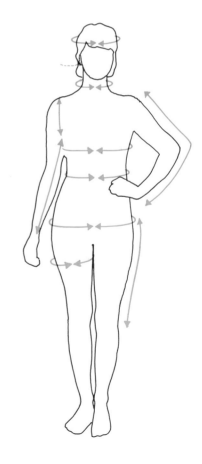

STANDARD MEASUREMENT CHART

This chart contains the most frequently re- quired measurements. You may photocopy it to use as a standard chart. Be sure to fill in the date when you take measurements, so you can tell if they may need updating.

MEASURING THE ACTOR

NAME _____

HEIGHT_____

CHEST _____

WAIST _____

HIPS _____

NAPE TO WAIST (BACK) _____

NAPE TO WAIST (FRONT) _____

ACROSS BACK _____

ACROSS FRONT_____

ACROSS SHOULDERS _____

SHOULDER _____

ARMHOLE _____

UNDERARM TO WAIST_____

SHOULDER-ELBOW-WRIST (BENT)_____

INSIDE ARM (STRAIGHT)_____

NECK_____

INSIDE LEG _____

OUTSIDE LEG (TO KNEE)_____

OUTSIDE LEG (TO GROUND) _____

SHOE _____

CIRCUMFERENCE OF HEAD_____

WRIST_____

FOREARM _____

ELBOW_____

PIERCED EARS_____

UNDER KNEE_____

ABOVE KNEE_____

THIGH _____

HISTORICAL RESEARCH

Historical accuracy can make your designs more believable, placing the action in a very specific context. It is obviously useful for naturalistic plays, where the more specific and reliable your historical detail is, the more convincing your effect will be. In this genre you are aiming to convince the audience of the credibility of the action and any historical innacuracies will quickly be spotted.

But historical research can also be used as the basis for invention. In neo-realistic productions the information from careful research can provide the foundation for your clever imaginative elaboration. Indeed, a good design often involves the recognition by the audience of the historical facts from which a fantastic creation springs.

In either case do your research with a designer's eye, adapting what you learn for use on stage. Your choices will be made to suit the individual personalities of the play's characters as much as for historical accuracy. Your research should always aim towards this end.

One word of caution: many period costumes were meant to be paraded in or worn on physically undemanding occasions. Actors are called upon to be much more energetic and need to move freely in order to perform. You will have to make compromises in both design and construction no matter how thoroughly you research.

WHAT COSTUME REALLY LOOKED LIKE

Your sources of information about a historical period will necessarily be restricted. The available evidence can be rather limited, and misleading for the following reasons:

-paintings and fashion plates usually show how fashionable people looked, or rather how they would have liked to be seen. The lower classes are often very unrepresented and frequently idealized in art.

-old costumes in museums or private collections can also be misleading. You must ask why they have been saved. They may have been kept after the unexpected death of their owner, but they may always have been considered unfashionably ugly or a mistaken purchase not worth wearing!

When researching try to get a good picture of the general outline, shape and construction points for the styles of any period. With this clearly in mind you will be free to invent appropriate detail within accurate historical information.

WHAT AND WHERE TO RESEARCH

There are many different sources for historical research. You will discover many of these as you use your library and art galleries. Remember to look outside the art and costume sections.

Here is a list of what to look for and some ideas for where to start your research:

General shape and outline
This information is best gathered from the paintings, photographs and fashion magazines of the period. Look for artists who specialize in pictures of social life, as well as for portrait painters. They will provide you with an idea of the general cultural background. It is important to understand why the clothes are shaped as they are, and the different customs throughout the class structure.

Construction
There are many specialist costume books available nowadays to provide this information. Some are necessarily very selective and provide only a generalized pictorial account of fashion. Choose those that have patterns derived from actual period garments, and supplement them with written or sketched analyses by costume historians. A list of useful publications is included at the end of this book.

Period fabrics
Be careful to note the fabrics that were fashionable. You can read about these in costume books but your best source is probably a costume collection in a museum.

Colours and dyes
An idea of what was fashionable can be found in paintings, mail order catalogues and surviving garments.

Accessories

You will need to be inventive in your research to discover all the details you need concerning hairstyles and make-up, shoes and other fashion accessories. Sculptures and porcelain figures are useful for the rear views of hairstyles. Antique sales catalogues and specialist collectors' books can tell you about watches, handbags and jewellery. Details are frequently hidden in the background to religious as well as secular paintings.

CHOOSING A DESIGN STYLE

The design style for the production will evolve from the preliminary discussions with the director. If more than one designer is involved, co-operation and communication are very important. Make sure that everyone understands the style you are aiming for.

Choose a style that will best bring out the mood of the play:

■ is it essential to believe that the characters in the drama are or could be real people? Does the script seem like the retelling of an actual event? If you think so, *realism* is the style to aim for

■ are the characters used in a story told to explore moral or ethical issues? Is it important that the audience focuses on what they represent rather than what particular social circumstances they find themselves in? With a script where you judge this to be the case, you will probably want to use an *abstract* design style

■ sometimes characters are exaggerated for comic or dramatic effect. We realize that they are not behaving as we would do in the situation but we accept the dramatist's convention and enjoy the theatricality of his

Realistic, Abstract and Neo-realistic designs for Oedipus Rex.

exploration of the story. *Neo-realism* is suggested by this kind of play.

Whatever style you choose be aware of the practical design implications in its use.

REALISM

When you are aiming for historical accuracy your preliminary work will require much careful historical research so that you become familiar with hairstyles, fabrics, colours etc. You will be choosing fabrics for their similarity to the authentic ones from the period, taking care about colour, weave and patterns. You may wish to use 'real' old garments or decorative details such as lace collars, braids or footwear. You will be using historical patterns and fitting techniques. The breaking down of costumes to make them look well worn will be necessary. Undergarments, even if unseen, will need careful consideration and use.

ABSTRACT DESIGN

This style uses its visual elements to express abstract and poetic ideas. You must take great care to ensure that you are using the 'visual currency' of your audience. Costume shape is chosen for its abstract psychological power. Colour and texture too become very important. Decoration is often reduced to a minimum and is of a symbolic kind. Even jewellery, hairstyles and hats need to be thought of in abstract terms. You will be choosing fabrics for their physical qualities – silks that float magically, felt or grosgrains for stiffness, 'shot' taffeta for its dual visual nature. In some cases costumes may be built over large paddings or wire frames to achieve an unusual outline. But take care that the costumes do not overwhelm the actors. Remember that the costumes do not do the acting.

NEO-REALISM

The roots of this style lie in reality, but the expression of the characters' personalities is in an exaggerated form. Heightened details on costume give the right effects. Unusual fabrics, sparkling or embossed, provide a sense of the theatrical. A character can be built up out of a wealth of decorative detail. You may wish to use anachronisms, including something from another historical period. Bear in mind that this style must have a recognizable reality at its heart. You will need a clear understanding of the period costume you are using as a base, synthesizing and exaggerating it. You will face difficult decisions about how far to abandon or stretch reality.

WHAT APPROACH?

The Greek play *Oedipus Rex*, telling how the King of Thebes uncovers his own guilty past, presents us with a choice of stylistic approaches. The importance of this choice is demonstrated by the different visual emphases apparent in the drawings shown here.

Abstract design

This style underlines the universal themes implicit in the story and its characters. Oedipus and Jocasta, the giant tragic figures of power, have costumes which emphasize their estrangement from ordinary reality. They are made taller by the use of platformed shoes and high crowns. They wear cold, formal masks. Their subjects, on the other hand, are a choric symbol of a blemished society. The disease is expressed in abstract patterning on their garments.

Realism

The emphasis in this style is on the historical Greek background. The poverty and disease are shown realistically through garments and make-up. The chorus wears the simple seamless garments of classical times. The King and Queen's clothes, constructed in the same way but covered in ornate jewellery, using designs drawn from decoration on pottery and statues. Hair styles and make-up are as historically accurate as possible.

Neo-realism

Although the costume ideas are drawn from the illustrations on vases and sculpture in these designs, the shapes are exaggerated to give a decadent emphasis to the robes of the protagonists. The drapes are extravagant, stiff and formalized. On the costumes of the chorus the tears and ragged edges are organized in a decorative manner to give them a unified menace. All the clothes are clearly drawn from real Greek styles, but adapted to underline and heighten the production ideas

PREPARING COSTUME DESIGNS

The most convenient way of communicating your ideas is through a costume drawing:

■ a drawing communicates atmosphere and personality
■ it shows construction detail clearly
■ all the information is together on a single piece of paper
■ it provides a convenient reference for discussion in the early stages of planning, and for actors to check back on as they rehearse the character
■ makers can find all the information they need on it, and hire companies can use it to search more thoroughly through their stock
■ drawing is itself a useful and inventive thinking process
■ above all the costume drawing provides a uniform goal for all members of the production team: actors, director, makers, stage management.

Of course, drawing is not the only method of preparing a design. You could use a photo montage or a photocopy from a book of historical costume. But these are unlikely to communicate the exact personality that you are aiming to reflect through the design.

WHAT SHOULD THE DESIGN SHOW?

Include in your drawing as much detail as you require. If you are prepared to leave detailed construction or decorative points to the makers, your artwork can be quite vague. You may only wish to communicate a feeling, an atmosphere that the character should evoke. Perhaps you intend to give more detail verbally when you discuss the work with the cutters. However, remember that you will have to take what you are given unless a clear instruction is available to the makers. If a costume drawing is to hold all the information necessary it must be very precise.

Do not forget that back views are important, and you may need to be just as precise about their realization.

ADDITIONAL INFORMATION

You can provide details in a number of ways. Written notes, photographic scraps, source lists and fabric samples can all be added to the drawing.

It is a good idea to mount your design on a stiff piece of card and to add a lightweight paper cover as a protective flap. You can use this as an area for additional notes or sketches . The drawing itself will then remain clean and free of accumulated scribbles.

A costume shown mounted on card with a paper flap cover. There are pencil sketches on the flap; fabric samples and hair-style references are attached.

CHAPTER 3

THE DESIGNER'S TOOLS

USING COLOUR

Becoming familiar with a colour wheel like the one illustrated here, will help you to understand colour relationships and use them in your costume designs. It will help you to mix paint and understand the effect of using one colour against another. (Note that there is a slight difference in the rules for using coloured light. Details of this are contained in the lighting book in this series.) You will also find information about the effect of coloured light on costume, which you will need to bear in mind at all times.

Notice how the colours on the wheel are placed alongside each other. They form concentric circles of varying intensity. Each circle contains all the colours of the spectrum in an equal degree of brightness. The further the circle from the centre of the wheel the lighter it is; towards the middle they get darker. Be aware that the lighter a colour is the further away it seems to be.

Primary colours

All the colours on the wheel are made from only three primary colours: red, yellow and blue. These elemental colours are simple and bright, and can be used for a very direct effect.

Mixing other colours

Mixing the primaries together gives us the secondary colours, which are orange, green, and purple. We can carry on mixing until we produce the whole spectrum. Each colour is the product of mixing the two adjacent ones.

Complementary colours

Colours directly opposite each other in the wheel are said to be complementary. When placed together they produce a very bright effect, but when mixed together as a paint they produce interesting greys. You could use the contrasting brightness of complementaries as a scheme, or you could make use of the whole range of greys.

Colour temperature

Tints are divided into hot or cold colours, recognizing the psychological reaction we have to them. This is a useful device for a designer. Obviously colours such as orange, red and purple are on the warm side of the wheel and blue, green and lavender are cool. But within a single colour segment, e.g. the red one, you can see that the colour red has both cold and warm variations.

USING COLOUR FOR PERSONALITY

Remember that you are trying to reflect mood and personality in your costume designs. You will learn to recognize the various personalities of colours and to use them to create a variety of theatrical moods.

We often describe a personality as cold or warm and you will want to underline this in your choice of the costume fabrics for a character. You may choose a range of warm colours or stick to various shades of the same one within a costume.

Use all warm or all cold colours to unify a crowd. You can differentiate between the personalities in the group by using the temperature varieties of a single colour.

On the other hand, you may want to introduce an exciting contrast within such a scheme by the occasional use of colours of opposite temperature for certain individuals. Colours have other aspects to their personalities. Some are hard and some soft. Look to the centre of the circle for darker hard tones and to the outer edge for soft pastel tints. Each colour has its own descriptive quality.

Do not forget that a character's personality may change during the course of a play's action. You can underline this development by a progression of appropriate different colours in the costume changes.

COLOURS IN HISTORY

You will become aware that each historical period has its own fashionable colours. The pastel shades of the early nineteenth century would be unacceptable towards the middle and end of that century. During the American Civil War certain colours were favoured by the society in the North and at the same time disparaged by the South. Take note of these fashions, particularly when designing realistic costume.

Much of this depends on the dyes available at the time. The bright acid colours available today are the product of chemical dyes. They look inappropriate in the costume of periods prior to 1910. For the most part, antique costume used natural dyes which have a much softer quality.

Choose your colour scheme carefully within a period and watch out for an inaccurate or inappropriate dye

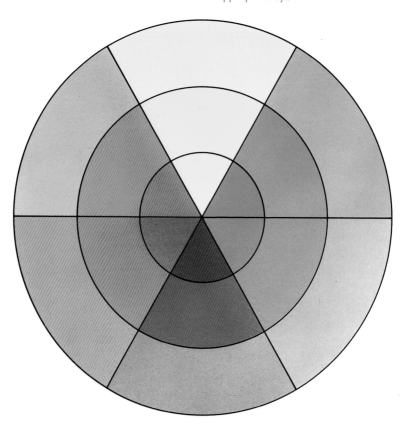

USING SHAPE

Every shape has its own personality and as a costume designer you need to learn to recognize these and use them in your drawings. Happy people are usually pictured as being plump, rounded shapes. Meanness is associated with narrow shapes and thinness. Take advantage of this kind of unconscious association to emphasize the personality of a character in the clothes that you suggest for them.

Even if the actor concerned is not the appropriate character shape, you can incorporate shaping into the detail of the costume in many subtle ways. Also you can use padding.

CONTRASTING CHARACTER SHAPES

Notice how every detail in these two costumes is shaped to accentuate the personality of the character.

Hair: one character's hair has a lively bubble cut; the other's own wavy hair is plastered down to give a feeling of conformity.

Collars: one is stiff and sharply angled; the other is a rounded lacy shape giving a warmer, more relaxed feeling.

Fastenings: Buttons and belts are a useful shape detail. Their personality will reflect that of the character wearing them.

Cut: notice how the same trousers are cut to a slightly different shape on each character for a different effect.

Shoes: design shaping is carried right down to the toe caps of the shoes and even the way the laces are tied.

SUBTLE USE OF SHAPE

You can use the effect of shaping in a very subtle way. Even within the strict conformity of a uniform, different personalities can be expressed by placing details such as buttons and epaulettes in considered positions.

The shoulders in the example on the left are built out by the epaulettes; buttons placed so that the eye is led up to them. Thus the uniform looks as if it is meant to be worn by a strong powerful person.

The other uniform is weakened by the narrow button pattern and drooping epaulettes.

The contrasting shape of each uniform hat completes the effect.

Personality conveyed through shape: disposition of the uniform elements suggests each personality.

CHANGING THE ACTOR'S SHAPE WITH PADDING

A tailor's dummy with a T-shirt on which layers of wadding are pinned, glued and sewn over the belly and shoulder.

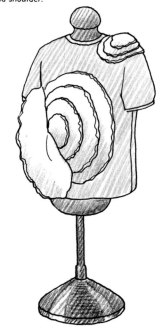

You may want to change the actor's own body shape to make him more physically like the personality outline of the character.

Paddings worn underneath the costume are easily made with polyester wadding. This is a lightweight material which is comfortable to wear and washable. Foam rubber is an alternative but not so convenient.

Create an enlarged outline in the stages shown here.

Put a T-shirt in the actor's size on a tailor's dummy.

Build up the shape of the padding using diminishing layers of wadding much as if making a geographical model. Pin each layer in place until you feel the shape is right, and then glue them together with dabs of latex adhesive.

Fix everything in place with large tacking stitches.

Cover the wadding shape with fine muslin or with another T-shirt a size larger than the original one.

USING TEXTURE

Even the simplest of costumes will benefit by careful consideration of the surface textures of the fabrics. Any garment must be thought about in terms of the messages that the audience will read through the texture of its cloth.

Choosing interesting weaves and finishes will give your designs variety and interest. You may want to juxtapose different textural qualities within a single garment, contrasting rough areas with smooth, matt parts with shiny ones. Using two textures within a costume will enliven it considerably.

Textures will also help you in your main duty as a costume designer: describing the personalities involved in the drama. You can say a great deal by choosing fabrics for your costumes whose textures underline character traits. You should learn to match the appropriate surface qualities to the mood or psychology of a scene or temperament.

Another way in which textures can help is in demonstrating social position. We naturally ascribe smooth silky fabrics to the rich, and hairy or rough ones to the poor. The textures you employ for a costume will quickly signal the class to which an individual belongs.

SURFACE TEXTURES

The weave or pile of the fabric give it its individuality. You will recognize the feminine smoothness of silks and satins, the luxury of velvets, and the coarse naturalness of hessians. Start to look for unusual textures, those whose qualities surprise you with their appropriateness. You may find them in plastic bin-liners, in old sacks or discarded candlewick bedspreads. By using unexpected but evocative textures such as these you will create a more vivid description of an individual's identity.

In addition you can alter the surface qualities of any fabric with a variety of techniques. Using glues, paint or special foams you can change the texture of a most ordinary material. You can add rough fringes cut from spare fabric or employ a variety of quilted effects using wadding. (See page 37.)

TEXTURE AND SHAPE

You can build into a costume surface textures created by the capacity for the fabric to drape or fold. If you gather a soft smooth fabric such as Jap silk it will create an interesting textural effect . A stiffer cloth such as a furnishing fabric will gather in a quite different way. You should take advantage of these qualities, using stiffer folds in materials for hard personalities and softer drapes for delicate natures.

CHOOSING FABRICS

When considering the choice of fabrics to be used in your costumes ask yourself questions such as these:

■ what texture words describe the personality of the character?
■ what kind of shape is suggested by these words?
■ do any textures suggest themselves which would describe the social position of the wearer of the costume?
■ can I use more than one texture within the design ? Do the textures placed together have the right effect?
■ what fabrics would have the appropriate surface qualities?
■ do I need to alter or add to the fabrics?
■ if my preferred fabric has the right surface but is somewhat insubstantial for the tailoring involved, can it be mounted on a firmer fabric such as a calico or stiff muslin?

CHAPTER 4

PERIOD CUT AND CONSTRUCTION

Modern clothes are made using techniques developed for mass tailoring. These methods are designed to make the most efficient use of the fabric and the factory machines. Dresses and jackets are usually constructed with simple side-seams and darts on the bodice, and sleeves cut with only a single underarm seam. Most of us are satisfied with the general good fit that we get from this kind of tailoring.

The history of garment construction shows the development of techniques designed to accommodate two basic requirements – efficient use of cloth and/or a good fit.

When fabric was scarce or difficult to produce, as in ancient Greece, it was used just as it came from the loom. The straight lengths of cloth were pinned, uncut and seamless, together; or draped around the body for the most efficient use of the material.

Later, when fashion was the province of a wealthy elite, tailoring techniques concentrated on producing complex shapes for ostentatious effect. Sometimes the fashionable shape was designed to show the fertility of woman by the elaborate arrangement of folds of fabric over the belly, while in other periods a good fit involved the body being hugged tight by the cloth and made to appear extravagantly elongated.

These shapes were created by a variety of techniques – with boned, flounced and padded underwear, and by careful positioning of seams and fabric grain.

Every historical period has its own costume shape, determined by these tailoring methods . As a costume designer you will need to be familiar both with the outline shapes and the construction for each period. It is impossible to imitate a historical garment convincingly without imitating the techniques of the period.

THE IMPORTANCE OF PERIOD CUT

By positioning the seams and fabric grains on your costumes in imitation of the historical practice you can achieve the correct shape exactly. If you follow the original pattern as closely as possible you will automatically get the best results. Do not forget that movement is often determined by the clothes you wear, and actors will often find an accurate costume a help in achieving a convincing stance.

You may need to modify the patterns for use in the theatre. Some movements are impossible in certain period garments but may be essential to the action of the play. You may be required to provide special fastenings and openings for quick changes. It is often impossible anyway to find time to do all the stitching and tailoring in a theatrical copy.

In all these cases you should adapt carefully to meet the difficulties while retaining the essential period shape wherever possible.

TWO JACKETS

Here are two jackets, one modern and one early nineteenth-century. The different ways they are constructed not only determine their individual shapes but affect the stances of their wearers.

NINETEENTH-CENTURY JACKET

This is not a working jacket: its fabric and cut are suited only to display. Notice how far back the sleeves are set.

The jacket is designed never to be buttoned up, but left open to display the elaborate waistcoat underneath.

Count the number of seams, especially in the sleeve and back. Note the side panel cut on the cross.

TWENTIETH-CENTURY JACKET

This is a practical jacket designed for comfort and warmth, and intended to be worn buttoned.

Notice how few seams there are, and how any additional shaping is formed with simple darts instead of panels.

THE CLASSICAL WORLD

The clothes worn in the classical period are very simple in construction. Men and women wore basically the same kind of garment. The short chiton, the longer himation, and the cloak called a chlamys, were each just a rectangular piece of cloth. They are characterized by their different lengths and by clever draping and folding.

Sewing was kept to a minimum and the garments were often pinned together. In Roman times jewellery was often used to fasten and decorate the garments, but Greek vases show little evidence of this.

Sometimes little fabric was used and the body was only partly covered, with bare arms, legs and, on occasions, breasts showing. At other times lots of fabric was used, as in the Roman toga which was made of a semicircular piece of wool about 20 metres (6 yards) long.

The simple hairstyles of the Greek women, based on buns and pony-tails, were to become over-elaborated on their Roman counterparts. The Greek men wore long beards and hair. This gave way to short styles and close-shaven faces, which the Roman men continued to wear.

Both Greek and Roman soldiers wore short chitons under their armour which the Greeks made of leather, and the Romans of metal.

Greek classical costume, circa 5th century BC.

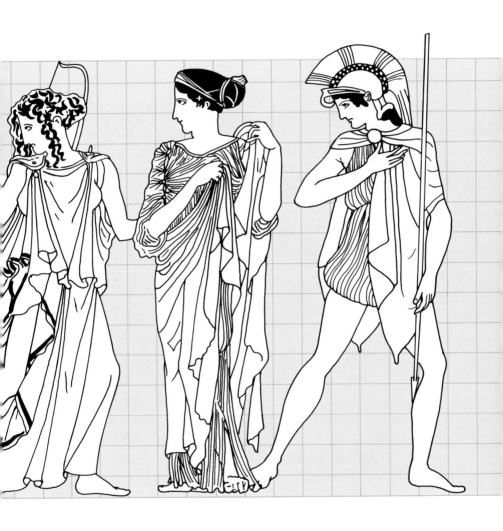

REALIZING CLASSICAL COSTUME

Although the classical costumes are simple, any theatrical version of them must be carefully constructed. The folds and drapes have to be fixed in place so that the actors are not inconvenienced or embarrassed by them.

The usual solution is to mount everything on to a simple undergarment, not seen by the audience, but used by the costumier to hold everything in beautiful, controlled shapes.

Antique pleating

One simple effect used by the ancient world is worth imitating. Antique pleating is shown on vase paintings and murals and is easy to do.

Take a piece of fine cotton cloth and dip it in very, very hot water. Start twisting the fabric from either end. Occasionally dipping the material back in the hot water, continue twisting until you have a small ball of cloth in your hand. When all the liquid is squeezed out, put the cloth to dry in a warm place. When it is unwound a beautiful pleated effect is fixed in the weave.

SOURCES OF INFORMATION

Mosaics and statuary of the period
Greek vases
Wall paintings such as those from Pompeii and
Herculaneum
A useful book is **Costume in Antiquity** *by James*
Laver

THE MEDIEVAL PERIOD

The layered effects of much medieval costume are used in different ways throughout the period. Many of the basic garments are developments from ecclesiastical garb originating in Byzantium. It is very important to differentiate carefully, and in more detail than is possible here, between the styles of the centuries.

The Romanesque costume is characterized by simple gowns with bold geometric patterns and elaborate heavy jewellery. The pelicon, adapted from the church cope, is an oval of cloth, often fur-lined, with an opening at one end for the head. Versions of this cloak appear frequently in this period. It is often worn over the pelisse. This was a long overgown usually tied with a girdle or belt.

The Romanesque man in his chain mail wears knitted stockings, leather arm pieces and much else that evokes their warlike society.

From 1200 the Gothic period shows a developing elaboration of costume. We see large sleeves on the women's long gowns, and simple wimples. The men wear knee-length tunics and cloaks over their voluminous shirts and stockings.

The Crusades of the fourteenth century bring heraldic patterning, hanging sleeves and close-fitting tunics for both sexes.

The High Gothic period (1400-1490) is one of padded and pleated tunics worn with tights by the men. High waistlines and long pleated sweeping skirts are worn by the women. The hanging sleeves show the fashion for 'dagging'. This was the cutting of the edges of costumes into jagged patterns and was much favoured by both fashionable men and women.

Romanesque costume, circa 1066.

REALIZING MEDIEVAL COSTUME

You will need to use your inventive imagination to produce the various forms of decoration used throughout this period. Even the simplest medieval tunic will be greatly enhanced by skilful use of bands of patterning.

You can paint borders with special fabric paints, cut them from other fabrics and apply them, or you can make up your own especially wide braids. These are done on strips of fine felt with gold paint, narrow trimmings, and artificial jewellery.

Heraldic patterns will have to be made by appliqué, screen-printed or painted.

Dagging can be a time-consuming process, with the cut edges of the fabric needing to be zig-zagged with the sewing machine. If you do not have the luxury of time, you should choose fabrics that do not fray such as fine felt and jerseys. Other fabrics can be painted on their edges with clear varnish to prevent fraying.

Tights can look awful unless the wearer has good legs. The unsatisfactory effect is accentuated if you use thin poor-quality tights. Try to aquire thick cotton ones; they dye easily and last longer. Do not forget that once synthetic tights have been washed in detergent, dyeing them will produce uneven and streaky results.

The outstanding feature of the High Gothic period is the headwear. Here are some ideas drawn from paintings for women.

Gothic costume, circa 1300.

SOURCES OF INFORMATION

The artists whose work will best inform you about the period are:

Henri Bellchase
Robert Campin
Petrus Christus
Jean Fouquet

Nicolas Froment
Hans Memlinc
Pisanello
Jan Van Eyck
Rogier Van Der Weyden
Conrad Witz

THE RENAISSANCE PERIOD

You will notice the regional variations in the costumes illustrated here. They differ for reasons of climate, trading patterns and other social circumstances. Do your research very carefully, taking account of date and location.

The list of artists included in these pages is long, reflecting the great flowering of the arts during this period. So you will easily find plenty of visual information. But be sure to back it up with research into the period cut and styles. Specialist costume books (see page 133) will explain many details of construction that artists have not made clear.

Italian Renaissance costume, circa 1400.   *German Renaissance costume, circa 1514.*

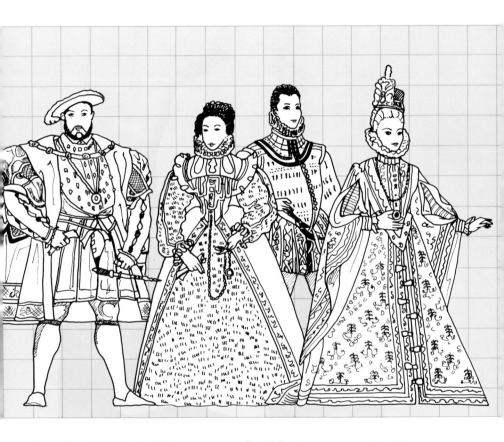

English Tudor costume, circa 1530.

Spanish Renaissance costume, circa 1550.

REALIZING RENAISSANCE COSTUME

You will need to use special construction devices, and take several short cuts in realizing the elaborate decorative costumes of the Renaissance.

Notice the gradual introduction and development of the boned bodice and corsetry. Some extreme examples are to be seen in the clothes of the wives and daughters of Henry VIII of England. It is essential to build bodices with the appropriate boned construction and to provide skirts with a far-thingale or roll support.

The effect of undershirts being pulled through slashings in garments is beautiful, but needs controlling carefully. Unless you fix the pulls permanently they soon disappear as the actor moves. It is best to make your costumes with the shirt fabric sandwiched between the lining and outer cloth. Stitch the pulled material in place through the slashings. The folds of the High Renaissance costumes should be padded with Terylene wadding.

The pleated skirts of the men's tunics look very splendid if each pleat is cut as a separate panel and sewn to the others. They then retain a firm shape no matter what stress the actors put the costumes through.

Very elaborate slashed sleeves and leggings such as are seen in German Renaissance military costumes can be imitated using a stiff felt for the outer fabric. This is easily looped to create the extravagant effect.

German military costume, circa 1500.

Sewn Skirt.

slashings fixed permanently

sewing lines

Braids attached before skirt is sewn together.

opening front + back for horse riding.

SOURCES OF INFORMATION

Look at the work of these painters for information about clothes worn in different countries:

Italian

Early Renaissance

Uccello
Veneziano

Renaissance

Gentile Bellini
Giovanni Bellini
Botticelli
Castagno
Piero di Cosimo
Piero della Francesca
Ghirlandaio
Gozzoli
Filippo Lippi
Mantegna
Verrocchio

High Renaissance

Correggio
Giorgione
Parmigianino
Perugino
Raphael
Veronese

German

Altdorfer
Baldung
Cranach
Dürer
Grunwald

Flemish

Brueghel
Patenir
Van Leyden
Van Orley
Van Scorel

English

Hilliard
Holbein the Younger
Isaac Oliver

SEVENTEENTH CENTURY

At the start of this period the major costume influences were the Spanish court fashions. High necks and ruffs were worn both by men and women. The bodices were elegantly shaped. Tight-fitting boned corsets provided the narrow support for the women's bodices and padding extended and curved the men's doublets.

As the century progressed, the stiffness was replaced by the elaborate fussiness of the baroque period. The jackets were more loose-fitting for the men, and worn with breeches. The women's corsets were shorter, their overskirts caught up and the oversleeves slashed from shoulder to wrist. The simple basic line was decorated with a host of ribbons and lace to produce the style we associate with the Cavaliers, supporters of Charles I of England during the Civil War.

In contrast the Puritans, who supported Cromwell and opposed the King, wore very austere clothes in tighter more restrictive styles. The dark colours contrast sharply with the plain but large collars and cuffs. They also wore their hair short, hence the term Roundheads.

By the restoration of Charles II in England (1660), French baroque fashions were introduced. The loose-fitting petticoat breeches and voluminous sleeves in male attire were finished off with laced cravats. The women of the period seem almost decorous by comparison, although their corsets are now designed to push up the breasts, and not to flatten them. The popular sleeve length now reaches only to the elbow.

Puritan, Court, and middle-class Baroque costume, circa 1620-1715.

REALIZING SEVENTEENTH-CENTURY COSTUME

The ruffs of the early and middle part of the century require great care in their making. There are two ways of doing it. The first involves catching an organza strip on to a neckband in a figure of eight pattern. This is time consuming but the result is well worth the effort.

The bullet pleating of the Caroline skirt can be done using curtain tape. It quickly pleats the fabric into even folds ready for catching to the base of the bodice.

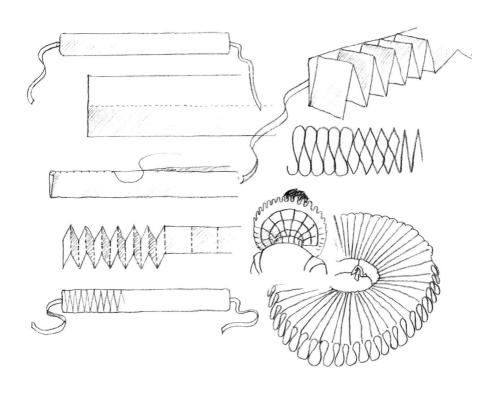

How to make a figure
of eight pattern muff.

SOURCES OF INFORMATION

Fashion moved from country to country at this period so check that your source is the appropriate one for the both the time and country you are researching. The following artists are good starting points:

1600-1620
Frans Hals
Louis le Nain
Peter Paul Rubens
Jan Steen

Georges de La Tour
Antony Van Dyke
Cornelis de Vas
Velasquez
Jan Vermeer
Zurbaran

1640-1700
Charles le Brun
Pierre Mignard
Justus Suttermans

EIGHTEENTH CENTURY: MEN

The long coats and periwigs worn at the start of the century gradually change shape over the next hundred years. The coat becomes first more fitted and shorter. It loses its sword-accommodating rear pleats. Throughout all this it shows off the waistcoat, which takes on a major decorative role. Eventually the coat is buttoned and the waistcoat only a short version of what it first was.

The wig loses its length and fullness, becomes a stylized white, and finally gives way to the natural look of the French *Directoire* hairstyles. The tricorn hat is a distinctive feature of the period.

Ruffs and frills abound, particularly at the throats of men's attire.

WOMEN

The all-encasing corset shape persists until the very end of the century. The front panel or false 'stomacher' is a decorative detail, full of embroidery and bows. Towards the end of the century the corset and bodice get shorter as the waistline rises.

The skirts are draped over wide cages and panniers for much of the period. They are parted at the front to show elaborate underskirts. Eventually the whalebone constructions disappear from beneath the dresses and the high-waisted ladies frocks of the 1790s are supported by underskirts which are gathered full at the back.

Ruffs and frills are used everywhere: at necklines, on cuffs and skirt hems.

Eighteenth-century costumes.   1725

1745

1791

REALIZING EIGHTEENTH-CENTURY COSTUME

There is no substitute for the corsetry and underwear that lies beneath the women's dresses. You must find the patterns for the correct shapes and reproduce them. Crinoline steel is available from theatrical suppliers and provides the best support for skirts. Corset boning is either the spiral steel kind or the widely available plastic substitute which can be sewn straight to the fabric. Always use eyelets and lacings for fastenings at the back of these dresses. Nothing destroys the authentic look of a costume more quickly than an inappropriate line of hooks and bars or, worse still, a zip. (These should also be avoided because they can fail suddenly.)

The men's coats need good tailoring and heavy linings. Try using toy makers' quality felt as a backing for the fabrics. It not only provides a suitable weight and support as an interfacing, but acts as a lining if chosen in the right colour.

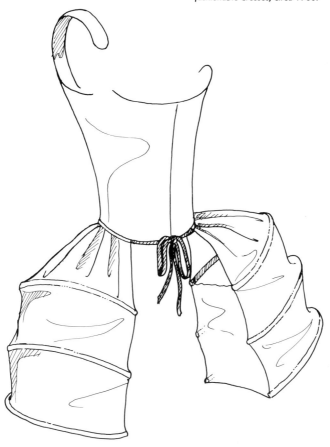

Panniers – of cotton reinforced with whalebone or crinoline steel – worn beneath the skirts of fashionable dresses, circa 1760.

SOURCES OF INFORMATION

Here are some artists whose work falls within the period and provides good reference material:

J.B.S. Chardin
Charles Cochin
Arthur Devis
Thomas Gainsborough
Hubert-François Gravelot

Francis Hayman
William Hogarth
Nicholas Langret
Pietro Longhi
Sir Joshua Reynolds
George Romney
Quentin de la Tour
Antoine Watteau
John Zoffany

NINETEENTH CENTURY

This was a century of revivals of styles. It opens with the imitation classicism of the Napoleonic Empire, a period of ladies' dresses with very high waistlines in soft flowing muslins. They have virtually no boning in the bodice and very light underskirts. The men's outfits of the time have high-backed collars and curved lapels on tailed coats.

The Romantic movement encouraged the gradual widening of the female skirt shape, until by the 1860s it was the familiar very large crinoline. The early leg o' mutton sleeve increased in width during the 1830s and 1840s, but it was to shrink to a close-fitting shape by 1870.

In that decade the wide skirt was replaced by a shape that depended on the exaggerated bustle foundation behind the lady. This was a time when fabric was swathed and draped extravagantly around the skirt, and decorated with fringing and pleating.

The men's coats show a move from tails to skirts. They are full at first but gradually get more fitted and shorter as 1860 approaches. Eventually the frock coat and top hat impose their personalities on the social picture of the late nineteenth century.

The development of men's coats during the nineteenth century.

REALIZING NINETEENTH-CENTURY COSTUME

Once again the foundation garments for the ladies need accurate research and copying.

Choose fabrics carefully avoiding inappropriately acid colours.

Add found collars or lace trimmings to the costumes you make. They add an authentic touch that modern laces cannot.

The men's neckwear is a feature of the period. You must copy it well: here are a few of the styles of collars and ties that were used. It is always a good idea to tie the cravat nicely and fix it permanently; contrive a simple back fastening. Then no matter how clumsy the actor, he will always look fine around the neck.

1810

1855

1874

1830

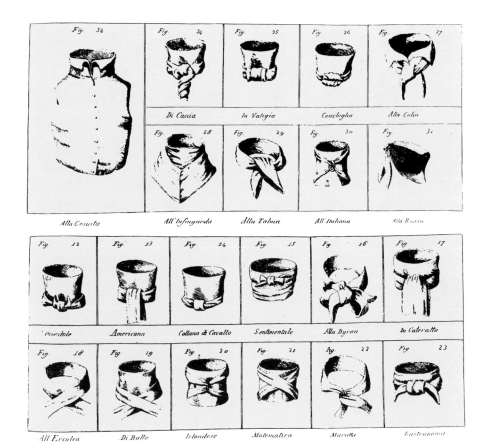

SOURCES OF INFORMATION

From the many available artists whose work shows a social awareness, you might choose some of these. They are listed chronologically.

Jaques Louis David
Francesco Goya
John Downman
Thomas Rowlandson
James Gillray
Louis Leopold Boilly
George Morland

Sir Thomas Lawrence
Jean-Antoine Gros
Jean-Auguste Ingres
George Cruickshank
Constantin Guys
Gavarini
John Leech
William Powell Frith
George du Maurier
John Singer Sargent
Charles Dana Gibson
James Tissot

CHAPTER 5

REALIZING THE COSTUME

THE PRODUCTION PROCESS

Having prepared all the costume drawings and agreed with the director on the ones to be used, you will be ready to begin realizing them. This process will involve the co-operation of many people. Your role will be to provide a constant reference point for consultation. Your advice and guidance will be needed by actors, makers and stage management. The way you work with everyone to solve problems and offer encouragement will greatly affect the finished set of costumes.

WORKING WITH THE ACTORS

One of your first jobs will be to attend the initial read-through of the play. At this first meeting of everyone involved in the production you will probably be required to present your costume designs to the cast. Remember that you are selling your ideas to the people who are going to be wearing them.

It will help if you can offer a few words of explanation about the thinking behind the designs. You should point out any physical restrictions that the actors may encounter in the costume, and alert people to any special corsetry or padding. Many questions will be asked, and a positive response from you will encourage confidence in the costumes.

Throughout the production process actors will be approaching you with ideas that occur in rehearsal while finding out what is possible in the costume. Assess each new suggestion carefully and try to accommodate it. But be prepared to stand firm if a suggestion is not practical. Explain your reasons to both the actor and the director.

The most important work with the actors will be done at the costume fittings. You will need to be sympathetic both to the requirements of the makers and those of the performer. Try to make decisions quickly but decisively. Any anxiety you show may inspire a lack of confidence in the work you are doing.

A similar awareness of actors' problems and anxieties will be required throughout the production weekend. This is a nerve-wracking time for the cast. They will need every support that you can give them.

WORKING WITH THE COSTUME MAKERS

Your designs will stand or fall by the care and skill of your team of costume makers. The best costumes are made when a designer provides the team with the proper amount of information, and displays a trust in the skills of the cutters and stitchers.

Wardrobe supervisor

It is essential to have one person to whom the supervision of the production process is entrusted. You may have to take on this role yourself. In larger companies you will have a wardrobe supervisor whose specific skill lies in organizing the realization of designs.

This person will have the responsibility for

employing the cutters, stitchers, milliners and jewellery makers. They will make sure that the fabrics are bought and reach the various departments, that information is circulated, and that fittings are arranged at times convenient to the director, designer and makers. Costume hire and the finding of those essential small items – socks, sweatshirts, gloves – is organized by them. A supervisor will attend dress rehearsals, and take your notes and their own in order to rectify problems quickly and efficiently.

A good supervisor is invaluable. Their organizational skills can free you to concentrate on design decisions.

Cutters and stitchers

The actual making of the costumes will be in the hands of the cutters and stitchers. They will be working from the information conveyed in your drawings but you will need to be on hand to answer queries. The more the team knows about the thinking behind your designs, the better the results will be. They will be able to offer creative suggestions about the construction of the clothes. Their solutions to problems will be technically sound and you should establish a relationship of trust with both cutters and stitchers. As designer you are the final arbiter on design decisions.

CASE STUDIES: COSTUMES BY FABRIC

It is essential that you choose the right fabrics.
Notice that every choice is made largely on the nature of fabric rather than its colour.
Materials are sometimes backed to provide stiffness.
Occasionally one fabric is laid over another for an unusual effect.
Fabrics are used imaginatively but practically.

A Shirt. For the require gathering and fullness a fine soft white cotton is best.

A waistcoat. For contrasting Shininess a Macclesfield silk or the reverse side of dupion might be used.

Breeches. Velvet corduroy will give proper stiff bagginess

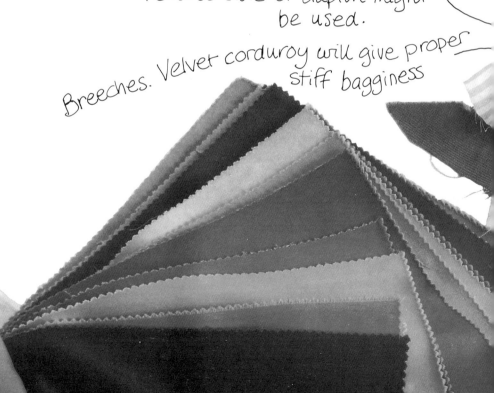

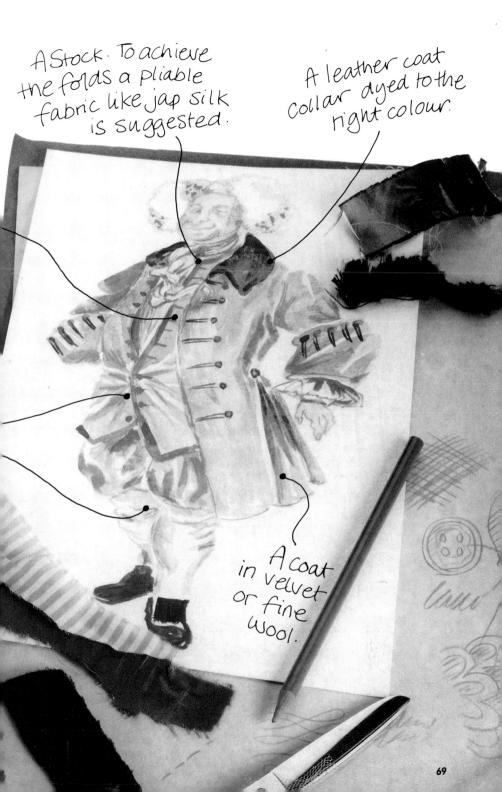

A Stock. To achieve the folds a pliable fabric like jap silk is suggested.

A leather coat collar dyed to the right colour.

A coat in velvet or fine wool.

FINDING FABRICS

Your first task is to analyse all your drawings and make notes about the kind of fabrics you think would be suitable. As you search for the right materials you will make some interesting discoveries, and perhaps change your ideas. Nonetheless, a preliminary list for each costume will keep the process manageable.

Your shopping lists should include details of the required quantities for every fabric. You may have to make adjustments according to the different widths of the materials you find, but these simple preparations will save time and prevent wastage.

SHOPPING AROUND

Try to find the most interesting and unusual fabrics that you can. A costume is always more attractive if the audience cannot immediately recognize the material used. A familiar favourite that has been in the local shops for many a month will be very unconvincing.

You should search out unusual sources for your supplies. A hunt through your local classified telephone directory will turn up some unexpected outlets. Look for specialists in silks, wools and linings, and for furnishing fabric stores.

Perhaps you have a local factory that will sell you large quantities or ends of lines. A wholesaler may be prepared to make special arrangements for a theatre company.

SPECIALIST SHOPS

If you live near a major theatrical centre such as London or New York you may be able to use fabric shops that specialize in theatrical fabrics. There are stores noted for their stocks of sequined and sparkling materials, and those whose silks are unusual and well priced for theatre use.

It is not essential to use these highly specialized shops. You can frequently find similar and equally interesting materials in your own locality. All that is required is the time to search for them. It is a good idea to keep your own list of useful and helpful suppliers.

A list of suppliers is included at the end of this book.

RECYCLING FABRICS

You should always consider using recycled fabrics for your costumes. It is possible to find very interesting materials in jumble or yard sales, second-hand and charity shops, even your own attic. Discarded velvet curtains, patched bedspreads, chenille tablecloths, lace curtains or table runners, even army blankets, are all perfectly usable.

There are several advantages in using old fabrics for your costumes. They frequently have interestng colours and patterns, they are already faded or 'broken down' and, of course, they are cheap. It is a good idea to start a theatre stock of such items so that you can draw upon it to save time in the hunt for suitable economic materials.

TRIMMINGS AND BRAIDS

You will probably want to add decoration to your costumes in the form of trimmings and braids. These can turn a dull or recognizable fabric into something quite splendid. It is worth searching for the most unusual ones you can find. Prefer ones that look old, are heavily textured, or can be joined together. Look at furnishing braids, cords and fringes.

All trimmings are expensive, especially if you buy small quantities. You will certainly find it more economical to buy 25-metre or 25-yard lengths from wholesale outlets even if you are left with a remnant to put into the stock cupboard. They will also supply buttons and other small items such as ribbons, so it is well worth establishing a contact with them.

If this is not possible consider some of these alternatives:

■ stitch together a common braid and a cheap ribbon to create something more impressive

■ paint woodworking adhesive on to a velvet ribbon or a felt strip and blow gold powder into it to make a splendid gilded effect

■ use plastic 'lace' tablecloths cut to shape for elaborate lace collars

■ create your own heavy fringe. Sew three strips of different fabrics together along one edge and cut into the opposite side many times

■ use piping cord as a seam decoration.

GLOSSARY OF FABRIC TYPES

Choosing fabrics for your costumes requires skill and knowledge. You will enjoy your trips to the stores, but the work is demanding. Always handle the fabric, feeling its weight and pliability and assessing its personality. Examine colours in the best possible light. Do not be fooled by neon or other distorting lighting systems.

As you choose you should pin a sample of each material to the appropriate drawing. This will ensure that you do not forget where they were to be used.

You will need to know about fabrics: their fibres, weaves and consequent properties. Here is a list of the most common types.

FABRIC	FIBRE	WEAVE	WE
Acrylic (synthetic fabric)	Bulky fibre used as a wool substitute	Usually knitted	Medi
Bombazine	Wool and cotton combination	Square	Heav
Brocade	Various	Square with a twilled over-weave forming a design	Varic weig
Burlap	Hemp	Square	Heav
Calico	Cotton	Square	Varic
Canvas	Cotton	Square	Heav
Velvet brocade	Silk or cotton	Square and single looped	Light medi
Cashmere	Wool of Indian goat hair	Various	Fine
Chiffon	Silk or synthetic	Square	Shee
Chintz	Cotton	Square and single looped	Medi
Crepe	Silk, wool	Woven in a step pattern	Light
Crepe, satin backed	Silk, wool	Woven in a step pattern	Light
Crushed velvet	Silk or synthetic	Square and single looped	Medi
Flannel	Wool	Square	Medi
Felt	Wool	Not woven but compressed	Varic
Herringbone	Wool	Type of tweed woven of at least 2 colours in an alter-nating zigzag pattern	Medi

DESCRIPTION
Not for dying – does not breathe
Difficult to find nowadays, this heavy warm fabric is soft and pliable. Use brushed denim as a substitute
'Self Brocade' means threads are all the same colour, but brocade can have a design overwoven in other colours
A very open weave sacking, with rough interesting textures
A plain simple fabric often dyed or printed
A heavy grade of calico
The pile on the velvet is cut into sculptured designs
Luxury soft wool, drapes beautifully but is expensive
Extremely light, soft, pliable fabric with floating quality
A cotton with a shiny glazed finish – often patterned
Good draping fabric, but needs backing when used straight
Has a shiny side to it and is more rigid than ordinary crepe
Wrinkles and creases steamed into the pile of a velvet
A simple woven wool
You cannot wash this fabric but it comes in a variety of weights and colours and is a useful backing fabric
A type of patterned wool

FABRIC	FIBRE	WEAVE	WEIGHT	DESCRIPTION
Jersey	Any fibre	A knitted fabric	Various	Jersey is stretchy, good for drapes and for close fitting garments
Lawn	Linen or cotton	Square	Light	A fine unstiffened semi-sheer fabric
Moiré	Silk or synthetic	Square	Various	A water-marked fabric with unusual lighting qualities
Nylon	Fibre used as silk substitute – synthetic	Various	Various	The most versatile synthetic fabric
Organdy	Cotton	Square	Sheet	Heavily starched but can be seen through
Organza	Silk	Square	Sheer	A silk organdy
Panne Velvet	Silk	Square and single looped	Light	A very flat piled velvet – very shiny – must be backed if used as a main feedback – good draping qualities
Polyester	Synthetic wool or cotton substitute	Various	Various	A dull flat fabric – cannot be dyed. Use only the best quality ones
Rayon	Synthetic Silk	Various	Various	A fabric that will crease and wrinkle easily
Satin	Silk or synthetic	Square	Various	Highly shiny surface on one side
Taffeta	Silk or synthetic	Square	Various	Shiny on both sides and glazed to give a certain hardness. Useful for linings when lightweight. A rustling sound when heavy
Terry cloth	Cotton	Square and double looped	Medium	A towelling fabric very useful for variety of texture
Twill	Cotton	Diagonal	Heavy	Woven with a diagonal for variety of texture
Velvet	Silk, cotton or synthetic	Square	Medium to heavy	Make sure that the fabric is used only one way as the cut looped pile shines differently upside down
Velveteen	Cotton	Square and single looped	Medium to heavy	A cheaper version of velvet

DISGUISING FABRICS

Sometimes it is difficult to find a particular fabric which is perfect in every respect. It may be the correct weight, a suitable texture, and the right price – but the wrong colour. On another occasion you may need to add an appropriate pattern or a different surface finish to the material.

There are several techniques for changing the personality of a fabric. You may need to use them on only one part of a single garment, or you could treat every fabric in the show to get an interesting uniform effect.

DYEING TECHNIQUES

You can dye many fabrics with modern household dyes. Different colours can be mixed together to get a specific shade. Follow the manufacturer's instructions precisely for the best results. Be sure to rinse out all the surplus dye so that it does not end up on the skin of a perspiring actor.

Some modern fibres resist dyeing so check by treating a small sample before buying all the cloth.

Dyed fabric always looks darker when wet. You can get a good idea of the shade you have reached by squeezing a corner dry.

Dip dyeing

Occasionally you will only want to alter the colour of your cloth very slightly. Perhaps you are dyeing a fringe to match a fabric, or taking the sharpness out of a modern dye. Dip dyeing is the usual method for these tasks. The dye powder is dissolved in a small quantity of boiling water but the material itself is not boiled. It is dipped in a lukewarm solution of the dye until the required tint is achieved.

'Scrunch' dyeing

An interestingly blotched effect can be created by immersing the fabric in the dye-bath while holding it roughly scrunched up. The random pattern that results is interesting in itself and is particularly useful for moderating an aggressive original pattern.

Ombre dyeing

If you hang a wet length of fabric with one end immersed in a bath of dye you will create an extraordinary effect. The colour will creep up the material creating a gra-duated coloured shading. This is a particularly useful method for ballet costumes.

PATTERN MAKING

Stencils

Cut patterns in waxed paper and brush fabric paint through to create a repeated design.

Sprays

Spray directly on to a material or through a stencil. A simple mouth spray is easily obtainable and can be used with waterproof inks, dyes or dilute French enamel varnish. A refillable aerosol spray (from car maintenance shops) is a more manageable device. Leather dyes in aerosol cans come in a variety of different colours and provide a more wear-resistant sprayed effect, but can be bought only through the manufacturers.

Appliqué

If you have the time, appliquéd patterns are a useful way to disguise fabrics. The usual method is to sew the pattern pieces into place. This provides a permanent, dry-cleanable result.

Sticking the pieces on with latex adhesive is much quicker but will only stand washing, not dry-cleaning. A glue gun is even quicker but strictly for temporary use.

Or try a double-sided non-woven interfacing. Iron it on to the back of the fabric first, draw and cut out your shapes and then iron them on to your garment. This is a particularly useful way of attaching appliqué designs to sheer materials

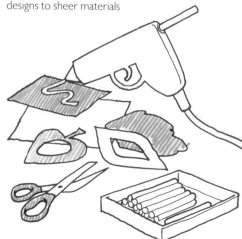

een printing with squeegee. Tracing wheel and cing.

Stencilling on pinned fabric with waxed paper and a short stiff stencil brush.

outh spray and leaf pattern pinned to a board.

Ombre dying.

A glue gun can be used for appliqué work.

Scrunch dying.

COSTUME FITTINGS

The most important times in the costume designer's production diary are probably the first costume fittings. Then the design stops being a two-dimensional proposition and becomes a reality.

The wardrobe workers will have worked to your brief, and endeavoured to recreate what you have indicated in the design sketch in outline, not yet in detail. But the fittings are the bringing together of theory and practicality. Adjustments will have to be made by everyone concerned:

■ the makers will need to adjust seams and hem lengths as they see their work on the actors for the first time

■ the performers will realize the restrictions or freedoms that the outfit will impose on them. They may well find the costume a source of inspiration, helping them to understand new aspects of their roles

■ you the designer should use the fitting as an opportunity to refine your ideas.

DESIGNING AT THE FITTING

Make sure that you have a good view of the costume in the fitting room. The usual practice is to fit in front of a full-length mirror. This enables you to stand behind the actors and get a long view of them. It also means that they can see what is happening and not be tempted to stoop forward to see what is being done. It is essential that they are disciplined enough to stand up straight, so that proportions and hem levels are adjusted correctly.

You will not be making design decisions immediately . Be patient – wait until the maker has made preliminary adjustments. They will usually invite your comments when they have done what they think is desired. Watch carefully and ask yourself some questions:

■ are the relative proportions of the garment correct?

■ have the details of construction been properly interpreted?

■ is the planned costume personality beginning to emerge?

Any adjustments prompted by replies to these basic questions should be your first concern. The maker will alter the costume and repin to your requirements.

Next you must consider the character effects you plan, and the actual body shape of the actor. You will need to make decisions about the former based on the reality of the latter. Here are examples of the sort of problems you might face and solutions you might consider:

■ actor has broader shoulders than you would like. The sleeve head can be moved higher on to the bodice shoulder

■ actress has a wider waist than you would like. Any vertical lines on the bodice (lapels, stomacher, decorative braid) can be sloped narrower towards the waistline

■ actor has short legs. Get the maker to raise the waist of the trousers and shorten the waistcoat for a more elegant line

You will need to be observant and inventive. Look and think carefully before you make your suggestions. Use your team's experience to generate ideas where necessary.

You will be asked to draw the required neckline, braid positions, lapel shapes etc. on the costume with tailor's chalk. It is easier to do all this only on one side and to let the costume cutter transfer the opposite shapes later in the workroom. You will soon learn to ignore the unadjusted parts of the toile and concentrate on the improved area.

At appropriate moments it is a good idea to ask the actor if what you are doing is going to affect his or her planned movements. Check, for instance, the restrictions as sleeves are fitted and as hemlines are pinned in place. It is easier to make arrangements for these problems now, rather than when the outfit is finished.

Fitting is an important part of designing and
realizing a costume. All those involved must reach
many crucial decisons in a short time.

THE IMPORTANCE OF UNDERWEAR

For much of the history of costume, fashion has dictated that the human shape be distorted. This has taken many directions: the enlarging of shoulders with pads, the distending of the stomach with wadding, the codpiece, the wearing of high heels or thickened soles on shoes.

The most remarkable examples of this are to be found in female dress. The various shapes and outlines that women have been persuaded to aspire to have largely been achieved by the wearing of specially constructed underclothing.

Because of this it is of vital importance that you imitate these garments correctly when producing period costume.

Fortunately much recent costume research has resulted in the publication of special surveys of underclothing. You will find it quite easy to discover not only what was worn, but a copy of an authentic pattern for almost any period undergarment.

CORSETS

The single most effective shape changer has been the corset. Its construction and design alters every ten years in the course of the sixteenth to nineteenth centuries.

Two kinds of boning are used nowadays in theatrical corsetry. The whalebone of the past has been replaced by steel spiral bones that are very flexible but firm. These are very strong and give great control to the corset. They are positioned in narrow pockets sewn into the corset.

The other substitute is the plastic version of whalebone. This can be used in two ways:

■ rolled up and slid into pockets in the corset fabric. You will get a very firm result from this method

■ sewn straight to the fabric. You can therefore have it stitched to a separate corset or straight into the costume bodice itself.

It is essential that your corsets have laced fastenings so that the actress can be pulled into the correct period shape.

CRINOLINES, PANNIERS AND BUSTLES

Almost as strange as the history of corsets is the number of ways that skirts have been pushed into odd and extravagant shapes. They have been draped over cages fixed to the waist, to the hips and to the bottom.

Without this type of foundation a skirt shape is largely determined by the fabric underskirt beneath it. The disposition of the pleats and gatherings, and the quantity of fabric used, act as a support of a particular design. Flounces attached at various heights push the overskirt further out.

You should be aware of exactly what lies behind the skirt shape you are tackling. Without this you will never produce the correct period outline. The best advice is to follow the historic pattern, and provide authentic underclothing.

Within 150 years Tudor and Elizabethan costumes radically changed shapes and personalities due to the changing shapes of undergarments beneath them.

79

CASE STUDY: HOW A COSTUME IS MADE

Seen here are the various stages in making a costume for *The Woman in Black*, by Susan Hill.

Initial design conferences lead to the preparation and approval of the design sketch.

The set of costume designs are discussed with the wardrobe supervisor and production manager. A budget for the show is fixed.

At the read-through the drawing is discussed with the actor.

Fabrics, trimmings and other materials are sampled, discussed with the supervisor, and bought.

The cutter and workshop team prepare for the initial fitting.

At the fitting the design is modified to flatter the performer's own shape and to achieve the correct costume personality.

The costume is made up with its decoration applied while the pattern shapes are still flat. A second fitting is arranged to check for the correct skirt lengths, the fitting of collars and cuffs and any final detail. Shoes are prepared, jewellery and other details assembled.

The finished costume is hung in the dressing room ready for the dress rehearsal

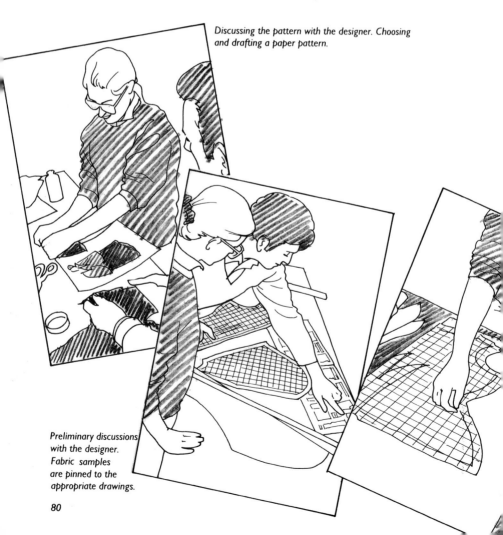

Discussing the pattern with the designer. Choosing and drafting a paper pattern.

Preliminary discussions with the designer. Fabric samples are pinned to the appropriate drawings.

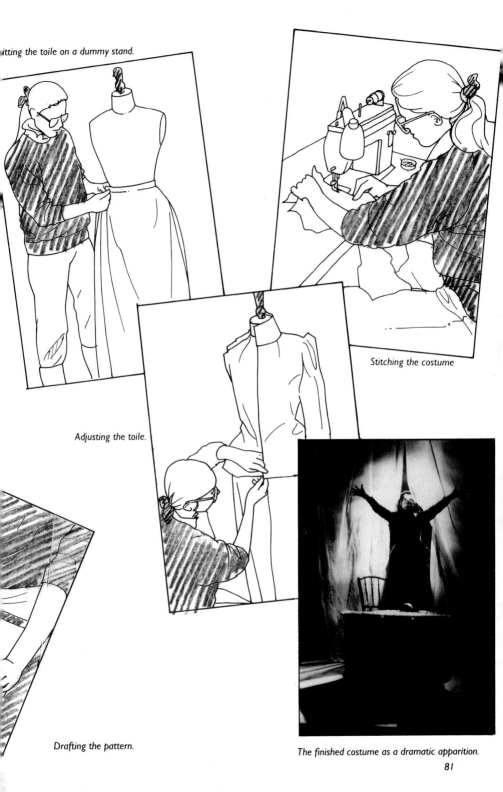

itting the toile on a dummy stand.

Stitching the costume

Adjusting the toile.

Drafting the pattern.

The finished costume as a dramatic apparition.

FINDING COSTUMES

Many productions, whether period or modern, will not depend entirely on specially made costumes.

Your costume plot may contain several elaborate uniforms or a substantial number of period men's outfits. You may find it more convenient or cheaper to hire these.

If you are doing a modern show you can probably buy the necessary things in the local stores, or borrow them.

It may be that your play demands clothes that are not chic or fashionable. In this case you should consider buying and adapting a variety of old clothes to look in period.

SOURCES FOR COSTUMES

If you are not making or hiring costumes you will need to be a resourceful shopper or a clever borrower. It is a good idea as a costume designer to keep a list of possible sources of supply for clothing.

Second-hand or charity shops often sell old clothes very cheaply; jumble or rummage sale clothing is even cheaper, usually pretty broken down, but ideal for certain types of play. For the most part what is sold will not be more than twenty or thirty years old. Such places are good for suits, dresses, ties, boots, scarves and many other ordinary things. With a little ingenuity you can adapt and alter things to a period shape.

Only very occasionally will you find a Victorian or Edwardian garment. Try to alert the staff to the fact that you are interested in any very old or unusual items that come in to the stock. They may start to save them especially for you.

Antique shops are usually too expensive to use, but you may be lucky and find a bargain or two. Keep an eye open in this kind of place for small items to elaborate a cheaper garment: lace collars, fur stoles, antique hats, lengths of unusual old braid or ribbon, leather or lace gloves. The addition of a genuine period detail will greatly enhance the simplest of costumes.

The larger stores will provide modern new clothes – but at a price! You may have to look at smaller shops or markets for bargains. Be prepared to add extra detail or remove fussy trimmings in order to make a cheap dress look more chic. It may help to dip dye something to give it more sophistication. You will soon see the potential in even the cheapest items.

Borrowing is another way of producing costumes. Try friends and relatives, and make enquiries at other theatres. You have a mutual interest in lending and borrowing each other's old stock.

ADAPTING OLD CLOTHES

You will quickly learn to see the potential in old clothes. Make yourself familiar with the costume details of the period you are working towards: the lapel, hem, and neckline shapes and the position of buttons, seams and pleats. This will enable you to recognize old clothes with the right potential. A few minor alterations can turn them into convincing 'period' costumes.

■ a suit can be made to look Edwardian by the addition of an extra top button and the re-pressing of the lapel shape.

■ check the vents and pocket flaps to see if they need sewing up or altering.

■ can you alter the width of the trouser legs, remove turn-ups, take out shoulder pads – or put them in?

■ adding velvet collars, covered buttons or velvet edging braid may help to imitate your particular historical fashion.

■ do you need to remove a modern 'tailored' look? You might consider machine washing the garment and pressing it back into a 'softer' shape.

■ your last step might be to break down the costume. A few wear marks and a careful use of sprayed dye will give it a suitable theatrical reality (see page 74)

■ his sketch suggests an Edwardian suit for the character of an old man. Using it as a guide, a suit is found which is the right size. With careful alterations the finished costume is a credible version of the original drawing.

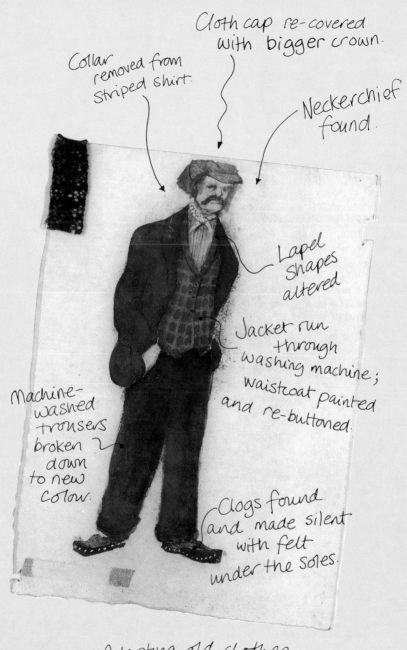

Cloth cap re-covered with bigger crown.

Collar removed from striped shirt.

Neckerchief found.

Lapel shapes altered

Jacket run through washing machine; waistcoat painted and re-buttoned.

Machine-washed trousers broken down to new colour.

Clogs found and made silent with felt under the soles.

Adapting old clothes.

BREAKING COSTUMES DOWN

Sometimes it is important that a costume should not look brand new. A character may be a vagabond living rough or a peasant. You may even wish to give a 'lived in' look to grand clothes to stop them looking like products of your theatre wardrobe department.

There are several ways to distress or 'break down' your costumes. Used carefully they will improve their sense of reality. The golden rule in all breaking down is to add effects only where the garment would wear out naturally. Some techniques apply to all costumes, but others have to be judged appropriate to each individual case.

It is always better to make the original costume as completely as you can before attacking it with these techniques. It will be obvious if you have skimped the making knowing that it is to be broken down later.

If you wish to dry-clean the costumes during the play's run choose the techniques with care. Some paints, dyes or adhesives will disappear in the process. It is a good idea to prepare a test piece of fabric with trials of the materials to be used, and send it to the dry-cleaners. In the same way you can find techniques which can be eradicated after the show finishes, and the costume returned to stock or lender.

TECHNIQUES

To give a costume a lightly worn effect you can simply send it to the dry-cleaners. If you can, let the actor wear the clothes in rehearsal for as long as possible before the play's opening. Both processes will start to remove initial crispness.

The most efficient way to age costumes is to spray areas of dirt into them. You can use a variety of different sprays:

Leather dye sprays are available in a wide range of colours and are resistant to wear and dry-cleaning. You may find it necessary to purchase these direct from the manufacturer.

Spray car paints are more readily bought but they wear off in time and do not resist dry-cleaning very well; suitable for short runs.

French enamel varnish (FEV), from theatrical paint suppliers, is designed for spray application. Use a mouth spray or a refillable air spray gun.

Work on a tailor's dummy covered with polythene sheet. Spray very carefully, building up your effects by layers. Only spray in natural areas of wear – the cuffs, edges, seams, elbows, and shoulder blades. Clothes dirty around pockets, button holes and all fastenings.

Other useful discolourants include shoe polish, glycerine, oil, soap and latex adhesive. Make tests to see what effects you can achieve.

You can add tears and scuffs by rubbing with a woodworker's rasp, scratching with a needle or a knife blade, or even cutting and tearing with scissors. Use these effects very discreetly and do not forget to spray around the tear mark to make it look old.

CASE STUDY

The final effect of a well-worn old jacket.

Always cover the tailor's dummy with polythene before 'breaking down'.

Tears in fabric simulated by scratching it with a knife or needle.

Smears of rubber adhesive provide a good shiny basis for soil marks.

n aerosol spray is a useful tool. Use it with weeping movements to get a blotched effect.

Brush on 'removable' stains like boot polish.

CHAPTER 6

COSTUMES IN PERFORMANCE

DRESS PARADES

It is best to avoid these. They are rarely the most efficient way of assessing what has been achieved and what remains to be done. At a parade all the clothes are seen in universal and inappropriate lighting. Some costumes are subjected to an unnecessary amount of scrutiny and criticism. Precious time is spent by leading players changing clothes, and known problems are rediscovered and agonized over.

It is far better to make sure that all the work is seen by designer or wardrobe supervisor well before the technical rehearsals. A list of outstanding work can be carefully assembled and added to during the production period. Encourage players to bring small problems such as missing or faulty fastenings to the supervisor's notice.

If you must hold a dress parade, limit it to large groups such as choruses or crowds. Leading player's outfits will be well scrutinized during the preparation period. As designer you are concerned with the look of the clothes as a group. Notice any misjudged colour that needs spraying. You may have to swop hats or accessories that are unflattering to particular performers. Focus on this kind of problem and make sure that the supervisor has a number of people standing by to take notes about outstanding sewing jobs.

THE DESIGNER AT DRESS REHEARSALS

Your job at the dress rehearsals is to be an alert and sensitive pair of eyes. You will be seeing your costumes for the first time under the planned lighting and performance conditions. This is a very short, intensive working period for you to make any necessary last-minute adjustments to these circumstances.

Remember that actors are under great pressure at these rehearsals. They are at the centre of a number of complex processes and you will need to be very sympathetic. Very often the costume becomes the target for any anxiety. You will learn to recognize this symptom and deal with it firmly and helpfully.

Lighting sessions

Attend these to watch what effects are being planned. Take care to point out any lighting that you think might be destructive. Coloured light will affect what you have planned. It is a good idea to have one or two representative pieces of costume available to put on stage. You will then be able to see how the lighting will enhance their colours and textures.

Technical rehearsals

Here you will notice how your costumes fit with the setting and work within the rehearsed action. You will face two main problems.

First, any movement difficulties will be discovered. The actors may find that what they have rehearsed is difficult or impossible in the clothes and setting. Address each problem very carefully. Find out *exactly* what the difficulty is and decide on the best solution. Director and actor will probably offer ideas which you must consider sympathetically before deciding. But remember that sometimes it is easier for the action to be changed than the costume.

At the same time, quick changes and the plans that you have made to facilitate them will be tested out. You will be surprised at how well most actors cope with these problems. What seemed to be a very short time for the change will be quite sufficient. If it is not completed on the first attempt, do not panic. Either practice will add speed, or you will be able to find different fastenings or under-dressing that will solve the problem. This is the purpose of technical rehearsals

Dress rehearsals

At these the lighting design will be nearly complete. Look to see the effect that this has on the colours and textures of your costumes. You will already have discussed the proposed lighting plot at the lighting session, but further ideas may need considering. You may feel it necessary to alter the colour of a piece of costume, dipping or spraying it a slightly different colour.

Also look at make-up under the lighting, offering advice to the performers if they have used too much or too little.

Take note of hairstyles and footwear. Performers will often ask if they are wearing a hat or cloak correctly; help them make any adjustments. These are the essential finishing touches that complete your design.

Make notes about anything that you feel is not finished or effective. Pass these notes on to the supervisor who will make sure that they are dealt with before the next rehearsal if possible. You will then be in a position to make a new list, refining the design by stages.

A big crowd scene needs special scrutiny at dress rehearsal. Take careful notes so that at the end of each run-through you have a list of problems to tackle. By the final dress run your notes, even for the big crowd, should be few.

ORGANIZING A TEMPORARY WARDROBE

For the care of the costumes during the run of a show you will need a special room designated as the maintainance wardrobe. If your venue does not have such a room you will need to organize a temporary one.

CHOOSING A SPACE

Find a convenient spot for the wardrobe: a central position is best, between stage and dressing rooms. Try to avoid a room at the top of a flight of stairs. If a lift is available try to be near it, especially if you have a large number of heavy costumes.

Basic facilities needed are: a sink with a hot and cold water supply for washing and dyeing; good light for sewing jobs; ventilation to clear steam or cleaning-fluid fumes; and electric power points for a number of machines. If the room has only one socket, get the technician to provide you with a multiple-outlet extension lead.

Make sure that you can lock up your wardrobe. Sewing machines, irons, spin-dryer etc. are often 'borrowed' or stolen outright.

EQUIPMENT CHECKLIST

Make sure that you have everything you need when you arrive. You may be too busy to leave the theatre once the technical rehearsals begin.

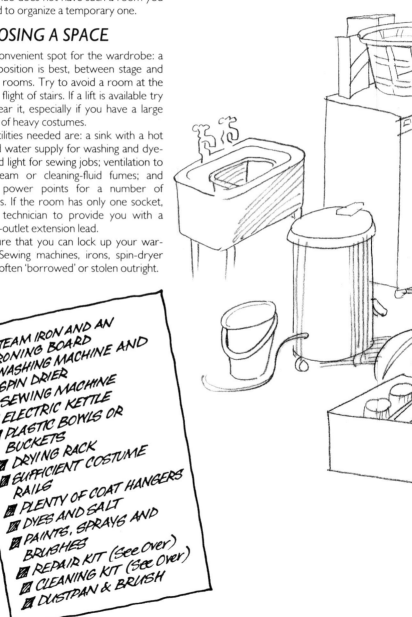

- ☑ STEAM IRON AND AN IRONING BOARD
- ☑ WASHING MACHINE AND SPIN DRIER
- ☑ SEWING MACHINE
- ☑ ELECTRIC KETTLE
- ☑ PLASTIC BOWLS OR BUCKETS
- ☑ DRYING RACK
- ☑ SUFFICIENT COSTUME RAILS
- ☑ PLENTY OF COAT HANGERS
- ☑ DYES AND SALT
- ☑ PAINTS, SPRAYS AND BRUSHES
- ☑ REPAIR KIT (See Over)
- ☑ CLEANING KIT (See Over)
- ☑ DUSTPAN & BRUSH

Organizing a temporary wardrobe.

CARE AND CLEANING OF COSTUMES

Costumes are subject to much harder wear than ordinary clothes. Even though they are worn for only a few hours in total, they become very worn. They absorb far more perspiration and vigorous action than everyday clothes. Make-up quickly soils cuffs and collars. So prepare for their care and cleaning before they are used in performance.

PLANNING

Make lists of which costumes can be dry-cleaned and which must be hand-washed
Collars and cuffs, especially if light-coloured, should be tacked into place so that they can be removed and washed separately.
Use detachable dress-shields.
Provide T-shirts to be worn under the costumes. They may need to be cut at the front so as not to be seen under an open collar. In very unusual circumstances you may even need to make duplicate pieces of costumes. For instance stage blood is very difficult to remove. You may need to provide two garments, the extra one being worn while the other is sent to the dry-cleaner.
You may need to impose a few rules on actors in certain costumes, such as a ban on smoking, or the wearing of bibs during coffee-breaks.

REPAIR KIT

Needles, cottons, button thread, elastic, tapes, pins, safety pins, fastenings
Scissors and seam ripper
Latex adhesive, contact adhesive, glue gun
Bits of the fabrics, braids and ribbons used
Iron-on fabrics, hemming and adhesive tapes
Stick-on rubber soles to quieten footwear
Inner soles, heel grips
Shoe-stretching spray or liquid
Hat stretcher

CLEANING KIT

Detergent and soap flakes
Dye remover and bleach
Fuller's earth (for grease removal)
Proprietary dry-cleaning fluid
Small scrubbing brush, clothes brush
Shoe-cleaning equipment

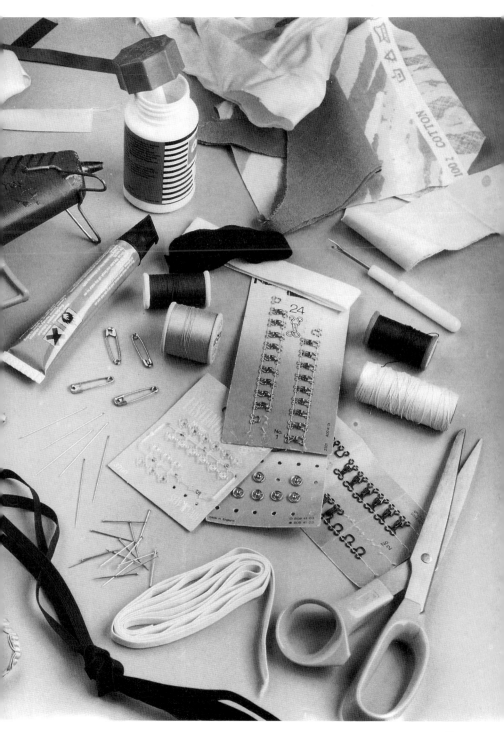

CHAPTER 7

THEATRICAL MILLINERY

Providing the right hats adds the finishing touch to your costumes. For 20th-century and some 19th-century outfits you may be able to find what you need in second-hand or antique shops. But for other periods, unless you hire, you will have to make many hats. The basic techniques are covered in this chapter, but you will need to be at your most inventive and creative when tackling millinery.

BONNET 1830s STYLE

Make a paper pattern, sticking it together with adhesive tape. It is a good idea to try this preliminary version on the actress's head, if possible over her wig. Use the pattern to cut the flat shapes out of milliners' buckram.

Sew millinery wire around the edge of the brim and the circular top of the bonnet – the sewing machine's zig-zag stitch does the job quickly. If the brim is very large you may need to put more wire across the surface

Assemble the wired pieces to the crown wall with large firm stitches.

Cover the bonnet with a thin, soft layer of wadding. You are now ready to decorate it.

Decide carefully in which order to cover the various parts of the hat. Try to hide any overlaps with the next section of velvet. Some seams can be hidden with bias tape which will stretch around curves and can be sewn or glued into place.

Cover the inner brim with gathered material and make a lining using the original paper pattern.

Finish the hat with feathers and flowers sewn to the outside of the brim.

Bonnet, circa 1830.

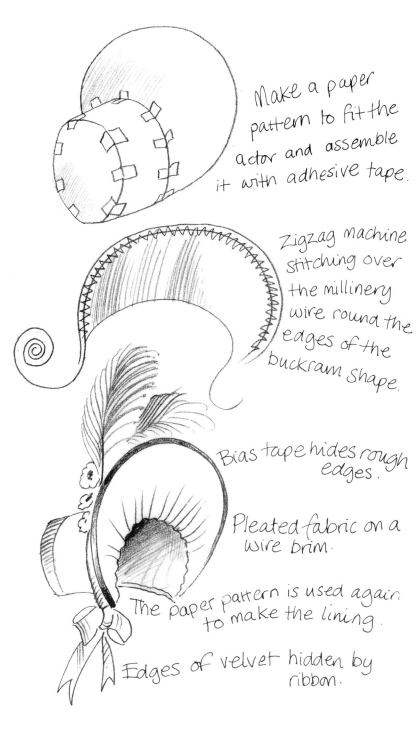

Make a paper pattern to fit the actor and assemble it with adhesive tape.

Zigzag machine stitching over the millinery wire round the edges of the buckram shape.

Bias tape hides rough edges.

Pleated fabric on a wire brim.

The paper pattern is used again to make the lining.

Edges of velvet hidden by ribbon.

JEWELLED TIARA

You will need a supply of special gold cord, coloured stones and sequins to make any jewelled millinery. These are available by mail from specialist theatrical suppliers listed at the end of this book.

Prepare a paper pattern so that you know the correct shape for your jewellery. Fold it in half and draw the design on one side. When you are satisfied, transfer the drawing to the other half of the paper.

Use a small-diameter hollow gold cord. Thread a hard millinery wire down this tube and fix the end with a glue gun.

Using your paper pattern bend the wired cord to the required shape. You will need to use milliners' long-nosed pliers and cutters.

Fix the tiara by sewing joins together as necessary.

Use a thicker wire to make a headband. Twist the ends of this wire around to form loops through which the wearer can pin the crown to her head. Bind the sharp ends securely with thread. Attach your tiara shape to the headband, sewing them securely together.

Stick on jewels and sequins with epoxy resin adhesive.

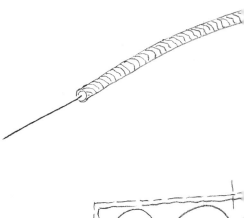

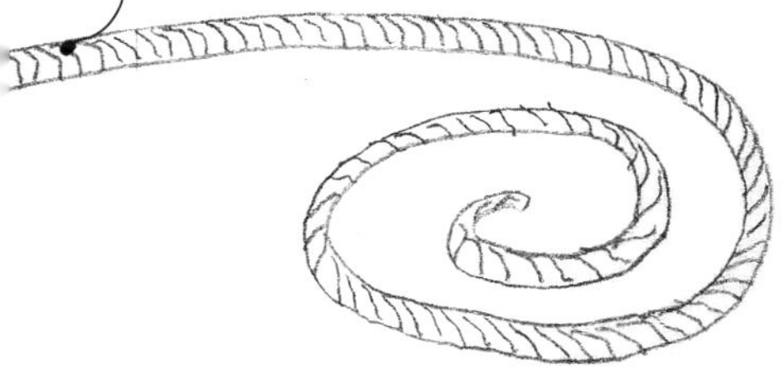

Thread millinery wire down
hollow decorative tape.

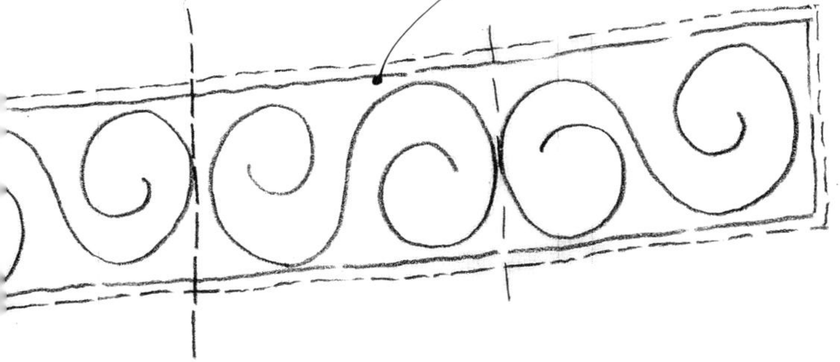

Prepare a
paper pattern.

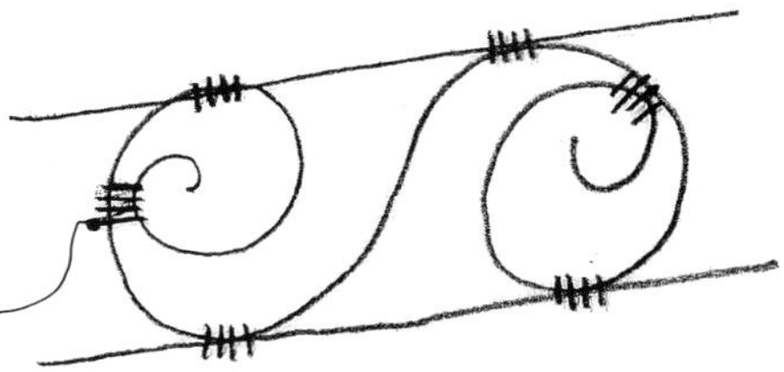

Sew the
ends of the
wired gold
rope
together.

BLOCKING A FELT HAT

Felt hats are among the most common and useful types. You can buy a basic felt shape and alter it to a modern millinery form. But here we are using a flat piece of felt to make 18th-century peasant headgear. You need a milliner's spring and wooden hat block, both of which can be obtained from a hat maker's supplier. The block could also be turned on a woodworker's lathe.

Use a piece of toy-maker's quality felt, dipping it in very hot water, and squeezing out all the liquid.

Stretch it over a suitable-sized hat block, holding it in place with the milliner's spring. Pull the corners of the felt down so that all excess disappears beneath the spring and the dome shape is absolutely smooth.

Paint this hat crown with felt stiffener and leave it to dry.

Using the block as a measure, draw the brim of the hat on a flat piece of felt, marking both inside and outside circumferences. Cut this out leaving 1cm (1/2in) excess inside the centre. Snip into this to form flaps to be glued inside the hat crown.

Sew millinery wire to the outer edge of the brim, using the sewing machine's zig-zag stitch, and paint the felt with felt stiffener.

Remove the crown from the block: slide a flexible hacksaw blade between the felt and the wood to release it.

Glue crown and brim together, covering the flaps with a hat band. Cover the wire around the perimeter with a bias tape.

Bend the brim into the required shape over a steaming kettle.

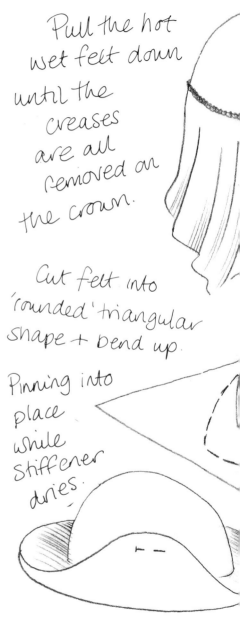

Pull the hot wet felt down until the creases are all removed on the crown.

Cut felt into 'rounded' triangular shape + bend up.

Pinning into place while stiffener dries.

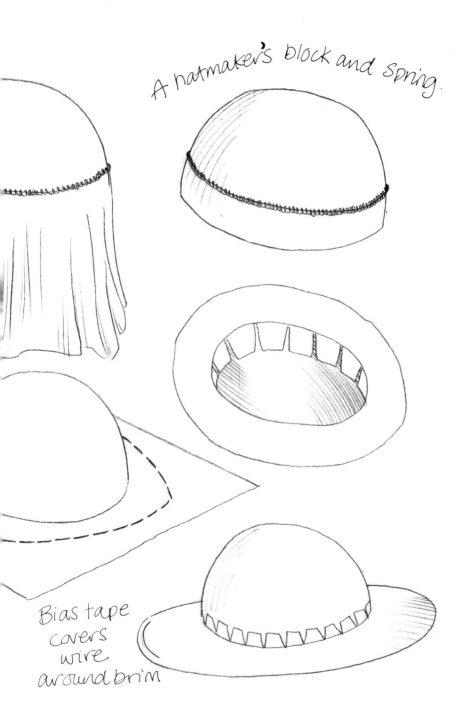

A hatmaker's block and spring.

Bias tape
covers
wire
around brim

MORE HAT SHAPES

CROWN

Make a paper pattern to the correct head size based on the example given here. Transfer the shape to milliner's buckram and cut out.

Join the ends of the crown together and sew millinery wire around the edges. Glue gold leather, plastic or paper to it.

Decorate the shape using gold braid or cord for the edges. Add sequins or metal nuts and washers glued together and sprayed gold.

Spray the inside of the crown with gold paint.

STRAW BOATER

With a paper pattern, cut the crown top and sides out of Spartra, a milliner's woven straw. Glue these to buckram shapes, making sure that you leave overlaps to join the pieces together.

Sew wire to a brim shape cut out of buckram and sandwich this between two layers of Spartra.

Assemble the hat, gluing and sewing the pieces together. Add a hat band to finish the boater.•

MEDIEVAL WIMPLE

The basic wimple is made from two pieces of cloth.

The rectangular shape is draped under the chin and pinned on top of the head.

The semi-circular cloth is fixed on top. Sometimes a wire frame, such as the one illustrated here, was worn under the top layer to form shapes like the butterfly wimple.

FRAMED SNOOD

Use cane or wire to shape the snood. Fasten the pieces of the frame together with masking tape.

Spray the frame gold and allow to dry. Hide the joins with braid and small sequins.

A boater.

Tabs bent and glued up

A medieval wimple with wire headband support

A Crown.

wire Zig-zagged
to edge

gold piping

jewellery

A framed snood.

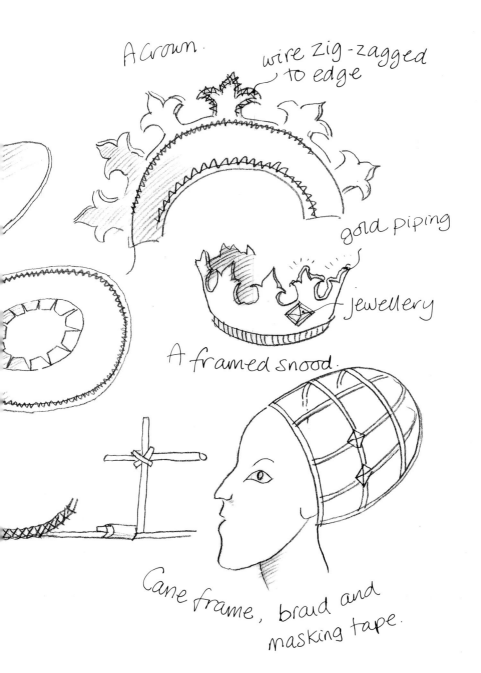

Cane frame, braid and
masking tape.

CHAPTER 8

THEATRICAL FOOTWEAR

AN IMPORTANT ELEMENT

The period detail carefully reconstructed in your costumes would be undermined by shoes which are recognizably modern. So take great care to carry historical accuracy right down to the tips of the actors' toes. Your preliminary research must include details of both footwear and stockings. Make sure that you have a clear idea of what was fashionable. You may need a number of ideas as shoes are always a difficult item to realize within the budget.

BUY, HIRE OR MAKE?

The easiest way to provide the correct shoes is to buy them from a theatrical shoemaker. But this is very expensive. Even if you can find what you want among their slightly used second-hand stocks, these suppliers are probably too expensive to be a source for more than one or two items.

If you hire a complete costume you will be provided with the correct footwear. It is hardly ever possible to hire boots and shoes separately. Even the specialist suppliers do not run a useful service like this. So that leaves only two options: finding or making what you need.

You will often find old shoes in yard or car boot sales and antique markets. A search in these and other places, though very time-consuming, can be very rewarding. But shoes must fit properly and your wonderful discovery may not be the exact foot size you require.

Your best source is inevitably among modern stockists. Some modern shoes are surprisingly suitable. The styles are convincing imitations of a variety of historical fashions. If you keep your eyes open you will notice many that can be used as they are, or with a very slight modification.

Unfortunately, modern shoe prices are very high. The latest fashions are probably too expensive, especially if you have a whole chorus to fit. Look at bargain stockists where the styles are less up-to-date. The cheapness of these sources means that you can afford to alter the shoes, cutting them, and attaching period details.

In the long run you should establish a stock of shoes for your theatre company. It will be an invaluable resource, saving you a great deal of money, time and effort.

HISTORICAL SURVEY

The following pages contain a survey of historical shoe styles. The pictures are a basic guide, and you will want to do further research in the sources suggested. A great deal of imagination and invention will be required to realize the styles adequately. Some suggestions are provided, but as you will be adapting from your own resources these can only be starting points to help you.

THE CLASSICAL WORLD
EXAMPLES FROM ART

Ideas for Realization

It may be possible to find modern sandals which are convincing enough or need little adaptation to be suitable. Here are some other suggestions for imitating classical footwear.

The Roman senator's shoe could be made by fixing a sole made of thick felt to a stocking, and adding leather strips for the ties.

The Roman legionary's shoe could be made from an old gym shoe. Careful cutting away of toecap and sides will give the appropriate open look. The lacing could be fixed through the sole and up the shoe's eyelets.

The patterns for the simple foot coverings are easily worked out. They can be made from heavy felt, imitation leather cloth, or suede. The lacing holes will need reinforcing with metal eyelets.

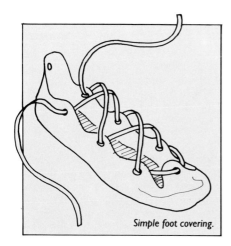

Simple foot covering.

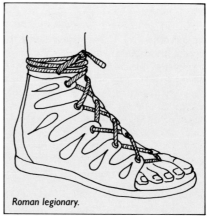

Roman legionary.

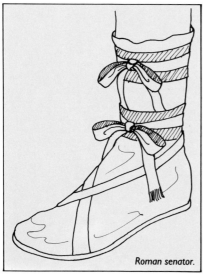

Roman senator.

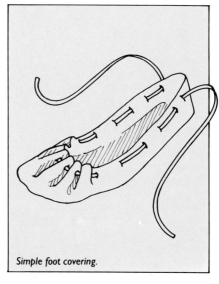

Simple foot covering.

MEDIEVAL PERIOD
EXAMPLES FROM ART

Ideas for Realization

Sharply pointed toes are basic to any medieval footwear. Depending on the vagaries
of fashion you may be able to find modern
shoes which will serve as a base. If not you
will need to be skilful in adapting materials.
The tulip boot can be made by careful
cutting of an old elastic-sided boot. A change
to a more medieval colour with a leather
dye will help the disguise.

Stockings worn over a cheap slipper and
embroidered with imitation lacing will make
the calf-length collar boot. First adapt the
toe shape by sewing a stuffed pointed padding to the end. You may need to fix a sole to
the foot to prevent slipping.

The simple cuts in this lady's shoe make it
simple to imitate.

Adding a cuff made of heavy felt or leather
produces the Ivanhoe version from a modern boot.

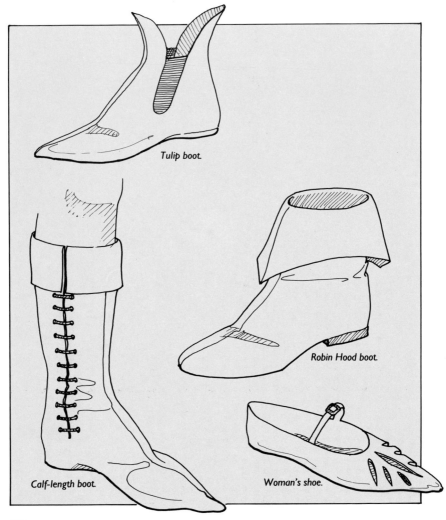

Tulip boot.

Robin Hood boot.

Calf-length boot.

Woman's shoe.

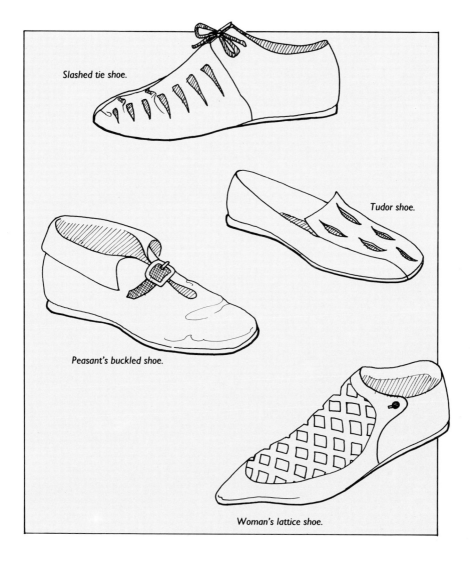

Slashed tie shoe.

Tudor shoe.

Peasant's buckled shoe.

Woman's lattice shoe.

RENAISSANCE PERIOD EXAMPLES FROM ART

Ideas for Realization

Once again, cheap slippers or old shoes can be altered to give a convincing effect.

If you can add a toe cap of stretchy material, such as Lycra, an ordinary laced shoe will produce the slashed tie shoe. The slashes have fabric of a different colour pulled through from beneath. These are best fixed in place permanently.

The lattice effect can be made as a separate piece of embroidery and fixed to a slipper.

The peasant's buckled bootee can easily be produced from a soft slipper. Add a buckled strap and a turned-down collar to complete the effect.

The men's Tudor shoes are simply made by adding slashings and broadening the toe shape.

SEVENTEENTH CENTURY

EXAMPLES FROM ART

Ideas for Realization

This is a more expensive period to imitate, especially if you need boots to complete your costumes. But elaborate and realistic period footwear can still be created by adapting bought or cast-off base shoes.

A modern laced shoe can be cut with a sharp knife to make the basic Puritan shoe.

Buckles added to a plain base are very effective in this period. You may find it convenient to thread wide elastic through them and to fix them in place.

Bows on the ladies' shoes can hide the sewing line where you have added the extra long tongue.

The nobleman's boot will be all the more convincing with the easily imitated cuff and toe cap additions.

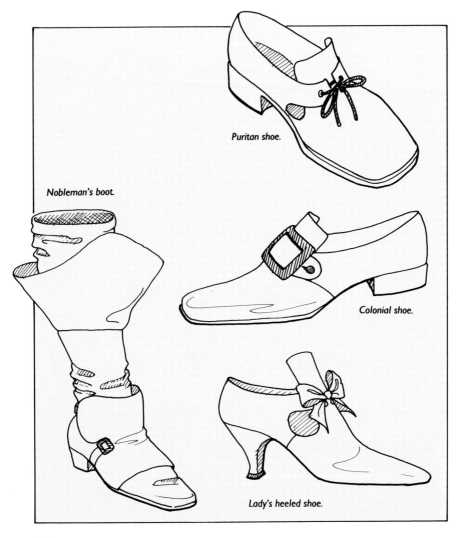

Puritan shoe.

Nobleman's boot.

Colonial shoe.

Lady's heeled shoe.

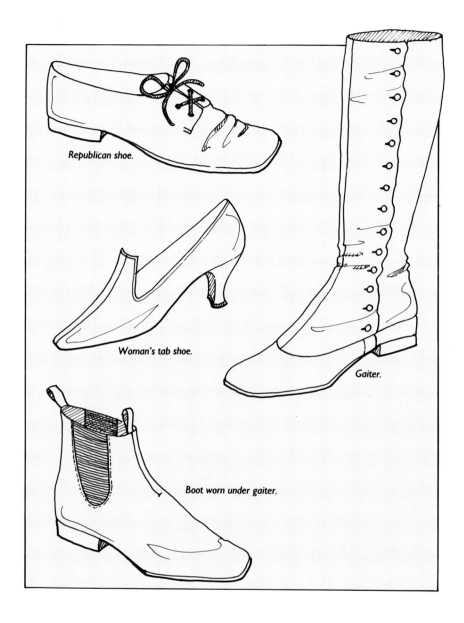

Republican shoe.

Woman's tab shoe.

Boot worn under gaiter.

Gaiter.

EIGHTEENTH CENTURY
EXAMPLES FROM ART

Ideas for Realization

The early part of this century is character-ized by simple footwear which is easy to imitate. The latter half of the period is also not too difficult to shoe.

The examples shown demonstrate how the early styles can be achieved by careful shopping and the adaptation techniques al-ready described.

Gaiters can be made from calico or leather. For a more perfect fit, or to avoid tailoring difficulties, you can use a decorated stocking.

NINETEENTH CENTURY

EXAMPLES FROM ART

Ideas for Realization

Early simple footwear like the Empire and instep bar pumps are obviously no problem. You will also be able to find some elastic-sided boots. Other shoes of the period will need a little more care and ingenuity.

The lady's bow-tie boot (about 1830) is easily imitated with a Scottish country dancing shoe and ribbons that match the costume.

Spats are not too difficult to make. They can hide an inappropriate shoe very well. Use a slightly stretchy fabric for a snug fit.

The high-buttoned or laced boots can consist of an ordinary slip-on lady's shoe and a decorated sock or stocking.

Man's French boot.

Spat.

Lady's button boot.

Buttoned tango boot.

Laced boot.

SPECIAL SHOE PROBLEMS

In some forms of theatre you must be aware of particular problems related to footwear.

FOOTWEAR FOR DANCE

Dancers are understandably very particular about the kind of shoes they can wear for their work.

Check with the choreographer exactly what is the most suitable kind of shoe to be worn for the planned dancing. Of course, you will be able to decide colour and visual style once you know what is required.

It is a good idea when designing ballet costumes to make the footwear exactly the same colour as the stockings to be worn. This trick makes the dancers' legs look longer. A different, more earthbound effect is produced with a contrasting colour.

All professional ballet dancers have their shoes made by the same maker every time to ensure a comfortable and exact fit. The wardrobe supervisor for a ballet company will know who to contact in each case.

CHAPTER 9

HAIRSTYLES AND WIGS

The characters' hairstyles complete the picture created by your costumes. If they are unconvincing they will undermine the credibility of the rest of your work. You should take particular care to make sure that they are well researched and as accurate as possible. How you achieve the period style depends on a number of factors.

SHOULD WE USE A WIG?

Even if a wig seems indicated, first consider using the actor's own hair as it has several advantages:

■ it is economical. Hiring a wig is an expensive business. A whole cast wearing wigs is frequently beyond budget limits
■ many modern theatres place the audience very near to the stage. In particular, theatre-in-the-round allows very close scrutiny of your effects and your wigs will have to be of a very high standard to be convincing. It may be necessary to use expensive film-quality wigs with their special invisible gauze at the hairline
■ actors often feel more comfortable with their own hair. They avoid the heat and discomfort of a wig and can feel secure in the knowledge that it can never fall off.

A little careful arrangement can often recreate a convincing period hairstyle. Heated rollers will be an adequate means of styling. You may need to add a small hairpiece, plait or switch to supplement the quantity of hair. Even if a colour specified in the text is not the same as the player's hair it is quite possible to dye or tint it in a convincing way.

Modern products are sufficiently refined to be acceptable to most performers even for off stage wear.

Alternatively, consider using the cheap, modern wigs widely available in local stores. If you choose a suitable style you can adapt these into reasonably convincing period shapes. Make sure that the hair is lively in texture, and pick colours that are as natural as possible.

This kind of wig has an elasticated base and consequently often has a hard hairline that does not look realistic if exposed. So only use them for styles that hide this defect.

HIRING A WIG

If you can afford to hire a wig from a reputable company you will be assured that it will be correctly styled, the same every night, and exactly what you want. Of course, you must make sure that in placing your order you give the wig specialists full information: an accurate set of head measurements, a specified colour, and a clear wig drawing.

Choose your hire company carefully. It is always preferable to have personal contact with them, so a local firm is usually a good choice. The best results are obtained when you can arrange fittings for the actor which you can attend and supervise.

Make sure that the measurements given to the hairstylist are accurate. Here is a chart to show how they should be taken. A good fit is essential, so include warnings about any special problems such as a very low hairline or an excess of unruly hair to go underneath the wig.

MEASURING A HEAD

1 From the front hairline over the top of the head to the nape.

2 From ear to ear over the top of the head.

3 Temple to temple round the back of the head.

4 Ear to ear across the forehead at the hairline.

5 Round the head (over the ears) from front hairline to the nape of the neck and back.

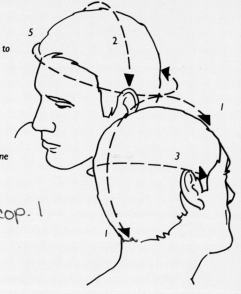

cop. 1

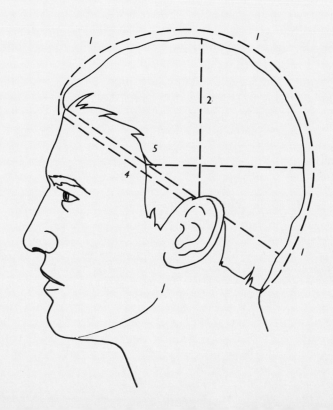

RESEARCHING HAIRSTYLES

General ideas for hairstyles are to be found in many sources. There are any number of pictures for every period but you will quickly discover that the detail you require is not so readily available. Consider the most obvious starting points.

PAINTINGS

Portraiture is an obvious place to start looking for information. It is a good source as the close-up view often gives you a good sense of the hairstyle.

But paintings such as these always flatter and what you see may be an ideal rather than an achievable style. Often they are portraying a sophisticated and monied class. Information about peasants and workers is unlikely to be included. Search for these in genre paintings with their scenes of everyday life.

All paintings suffer from a lack of a three-dimensional view. You may have to invent what happens behind the head. Pictures showing how the hair is styled at the rear are rare.

PHOTOGRAPHS

For late 19th- and 20th-century hairstyles photographs are a very good research area. They show a wide range of classes and the people are frequently not shown in posed positions. The information is often unedited and you can see exactly how the hair looked rather than what the style was supposed to be.

SCULPTURE

Sculpture is an ideal way of finding out about hairstyles. You should make a habit of inspecting the rear view of every sculpture you look at. Not only will you be able to see how the hair is curled and plaited, but you will often get information about the fixings used. Details of combs, ribbons, and pins are often included. It is a pity that sculpture is not more readily available to costume designers' scrutiny.

TEXTBOOKS

Several specialist costume books contain rudimentary information about hairstyles. You will get a general impression of the period from them. By far the most detailed study is by the American make-up artist and writer Richard Corson. His book *Fashions in Hair* is very comprehensive. It contains many line drawings for every period. Be sure, when using it, to check the index for the reference the author has used. Some styles are specific to particular regions or countries.

PREPARING A WIG DRAWING

You will be required to do wig drawings for the hiring company. Bear in mind that you are continuing the design process in the hair of the character. So put as much personality into this detail as you have elsewhere. Do not get lost in historical accuracy. The wig specialist will want to match the characterization you include.

Do not send the drawing away before you have shown it to both the director and the actor who will be wearing it. Discuss it with them carefully. It is easier to alter a drawing than a wig.

The stylist will need a clear, accurate drawing. You can present your information in a variety of ways: line drawing, photograph, or copy of the costume design. It is a good idea to include both a front and a side view of the head. Notes on the drawing can add supplementary information such as particular fittings, general characterization and, of course, colour.

You will also need to do sketches of facial hair – moustaches, beards and sideburns. Include a clipping of the actor's own hair for matching.

CHAPTER 10

THE ART OF MAKE-UP

USE AND ABUSE

Nothing reveals an amateurish attitude in the theatre more clearly than the misuse of make-up. Elaborately painted faces are old-fashioned; theatrical styles and methods have emphasized naturalism for decades. Very heavy make-up belongs to the picture-frame theatre which distanced the actor from the audience. Today, performers and directors seek to break down this division, and to form as much contact as possible with their audience.

Since the 1960s, make-up has been seen as a valuable aid, and not as a necessity. Actors will use it only when necessary and with as much discretion as possible. They use it out of choice, not obligation, to help achieve a particular effect or to overcome a drawback.

This change has been reinforced by the advances made in the technology used in the theatre. Today's lighting equipment has removed the necessity for heavy make-up. The halogen lamps now used throw a clear sharp light which removes the need to reinforce facial detail by painting with make-up. There is no need for those orange bases and heavy eyelining.

Of course, there is still a place for make-up. It can be necessary for fantasy or caricature. A play with actors dressed as animals or clowns will obviously need it. But before using it for any other kind of drama you should examine whether it is really needed.

WHEN TO USE MAKE-UP

Large auditoria

If your theatre is extremely large you will obviously consider using make-up to boost the features of the actors so that they can be seen at the back of the upper balcony. Extra lining and shadowing may do this job. You could deepen eye sockets with shadow colours, hollow out cheeks and pick out lip colours.

But be careful. Never overdo it. A good general rule is that if your means can be seen by the second or third row of patrons the effect is too heavy. It is a mistake to destroy the reality of the performance for anyone at the front of your audience. Check what is proposed at the dress rehearsals and modify accordingly.

Garish lighting

While most modern lighting does not require the use of make-up, some occasions may still demand it. If the lighting is very garishly coloured with intense filters you may need to sculpt the faces of your performers. Sometimes very directional lighting will require the same consideration. Careful use of shading and highlighting will compensate for one-sided or over-coloured effects.

SPECIAL EFFECTS

The main function of make-up nowadays is to achieve a necessary special effect. Sometimes it is essential to change the face of the actor with careful modelling techniques.

Ageing

You will most often need to age an actor. Although the trend nowadays is to cast people according to type, with young and old people in appropriate parts this is not always possible; also the character may age during the play. So you will be asked to provide make-up designs to age an actor.

Historical accuracy

Styles in make-up have changed radically over the centuries. As materials have been discovered and refined, their methods of application and use have altered. Every age has its own look. Sometimes the emphasis is on the eyes, sometimes on the lips. A pale skin or a deep tan may be in fashion. Getting these effects right for the period you are working with can greatly enhance your costume designs.

Researching these historical styles in make-up demands care and skill. You may get information from Richard Corson's book *Fashions in Make-up*, but if you cannot locate it, look at paintings. Analyse them to discover where the emphasis is being placed, what distortions of features are being used, and what lies behind the fashions. If you do this correctly you will be able to suggest a convincing period make-up to complete your costume design.

ALTERING A FACE

These two faces are exactly the same shape and size. Study them to see how skilful use of shading and the emphasis of highlights has effected a dramatic change. The possibilities for sculpting a face with this simple method are endless.

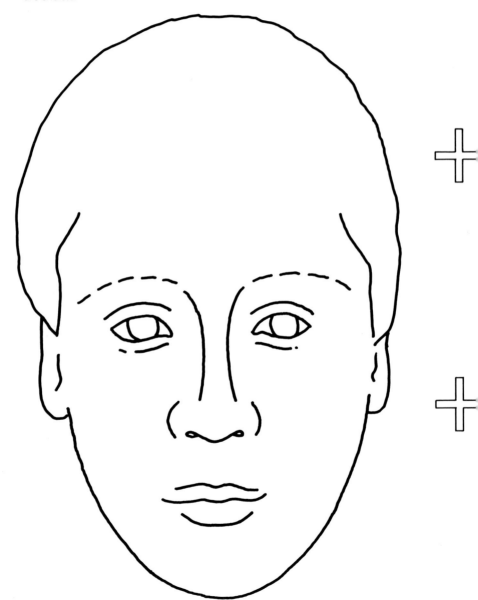

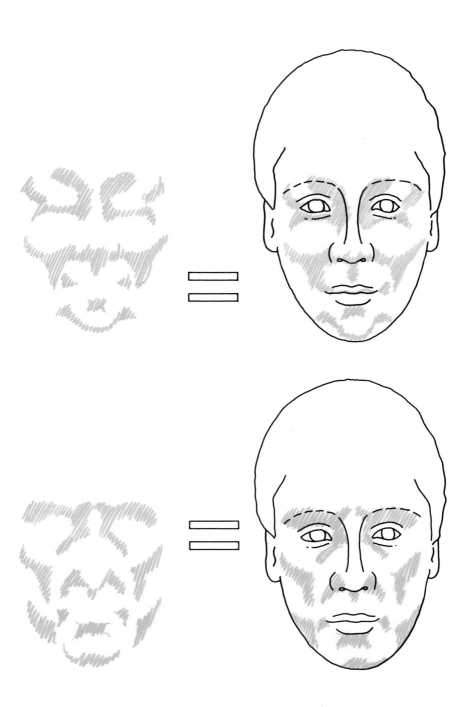

BASIC MAKE-UP KIT

There is no need to be too ambitious with your make-up kit at the outset. You will use very little, so familiarize yourself with the basic types before buying too much. Accessories needed are cotton wool and tissues, a clean towel, some sponges and brushes, and a mirror.

The available range of make-up is bewildering. There are several different manufacturers whose products vary in both name and nature. Feel free to pick and choose. There is no advantage in sticking to the products of one company. Use whichever you think will do the job properly.

Cake make-up
You apply this greaseless make-up with a damp sponge. It comes in plastic cases or jars, and in a wide range of colours. It is clean to use, fairly easy to apply, and gives a very smooth foundation.

Creme make-up
This is a velvety, non-greasy make-up that is as easy to remove as greasepaint, without its inherent greasiness. A little neutral powder over the creme-make up is necessary to remove its natural sheen. It is applied with the fingers or with a brush.

Greasepaint
The traditional basic foundation paint is used to give the desired skin tone. It comes in a variety of colours and in either hard stick form or, with a softer consistency, in jars and tubes. Greasepaint colours are easily mixed and they can be used to cover skin blemishes and the joins in prosthetic devices. It is also inexpensive. However it can be messy, rubbing off quite easily on clothes, and requiring powdering.

Stronger colours in stick form are called liners, or shading colours. They are a convenient way of painting lines, highlights, lip colours, and shadows.

Make-up pencils
Available in a wide variety of colours, these wooden pencils are filled with greasepaint. They are a good means of drawing lines and darkening eyebrows. Sharpen them with a flat knife or blade.

Mascara
This is used for darkening eyelashes and sometimes the hair.

Eyeshadow
This comes in a variety of colours but can be improvised with ordinary shading tints.

Face powders
To fix the basic foundation colour a face powder is brushed over it. You do not need a special colour. A neutral transparent shade is best as it does not distort the painted detail on the face.

Hair whiteners
Liquid or solid whitener is used for greying the hair. It is brushed or combed on, and is removed with soap and water.

Make-up removers
Cleansing creams are available from all manufacturers and also from pharmacies and cosmetic counters. Remove greasepaint or creme make-up with messy liquid paraffin, or with a pleasant cold cream. Baby oil is another alternative. Cake make-up comes off with soap and water.

Adhesives
Spirit gum is used to attach moustaches, beards, and the front lace of wigs. It is now possible to buy a water-based 'spirit' gum.

HOW TO USE MAKE-UP

There are three basic stages: applying a foundation, modelling with highlights and shadows and adding the finishing touches.

FOUNDATION

Cake make-up is applied with a damp (not wet)sponge. Stroke the face lightly until the whole area is covered with a thin film of paint. You do not need to powder.

Creme make-up is applied with the fingers, brush or sponge. Use whichever you prefer, but only apply a thin layer to colour the skin.

Greasepaint in a tube or jar is applied on your finger tips. Your face should be as greaseless as possible beforehand.

If using the hard greasepaint sticks, mix colours in the palm of your hand. This is a better way of ensuring the right colour than blending together random blobs applied directly to your face. First get your face slightly greasy with a film of cold cream. When you have mixed the desired tone, rub your palms together and transfer the paint to your face in a thin layer using a smooth wiping action.

Whichever sort of foundation you use make sure that you reach every part of the face, right up to the hairline and down the neck.

HIGHLIGHTS AND SHADOWS

If using cake or creme make-up, apply these with brushes over the foundation colour. Work with the darkest tone first, cleaning out your brush before blending the edges of the shadows into the skin tones. Add highlights alongside the dark areas to give the sculpted effects. Never try to put highlight on top of a shadow colour as you will usually end up with a muddy result.

If using greasepaint sticks, apply shadows and highlights directly or with a brush or wooden toothpick. Then blend them into the foundation with your fingertips. Highlights will be difficult if you have used too heavy a base.

Use highlights and shadows very carefully. They should be so subtly blended that the audience is unaware of the way the effect has been achieved.

FINISHING TOUCHES

Eyeshadow, mascara and rouge, if required, are all added to the make-up before the face is powdered to fix the painting. Cake and creme make-up rouges are applied with a sponge. Use your fingers with greasepaint.

AGEING A FACE

In youth we all have firm facial muscles and elastic skin. As we age, the sagging muscles begin to reveal the underlying bone structure and its hollows. It is therefore important to understand what the underlying geography of the face is before trying to age it. Take a few moments to feel where your skull protrudes beneath your flesh, so that you will be able to model the highlights suggested in this example of an ageing make-up on your own face.

Foundation: paler than usual in colour, more yellow and lifeless.

Shadow: light brick red with a little grey mixed in.

Highlights: white on the cheekbones and chin.

Nose: narrowed with the shadow and highlight colours.

Cheek-bones: shadowed and given a highlight.

Eye wrinkles: carefully drawn with the make-up brush. They also have a white emphasis.

Mouth: aged by reducing the lip width and turning down the corners.

Eyelids: lit with a yellowish paint to make them appear hooded.

Study old faces before tackling the job of making your own face older. You will soon learn to observe how people's features relax and sag with age. The hollows and lines formed by this process can be imitated with shadows and highlights as described on the following pages.

Make a collection of photographs of old faces like the ones shown here. Analyse them for highlit areas and for shadows. The broad planes indicated in these examples, when painted with dark and light make-up, will form the proper basis for an ageing make-up. Do not rely solely on lines. These should be added to a make-up as a last step. If you tackle the painting of an old face in this way it will be more convincing, and not superficial.

FALSE FEATURES

Unless it is absolutely essential do not use false noses, bald heads or any other form of prosthesis. If used unnecessarily they are merely a mask to hide behind. Good actors do not need the support of anonymity to give a fine performance.

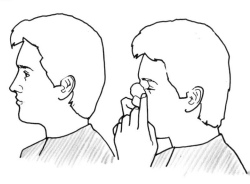

CHANGING A NOSE

This is done with nose putty, a sticky pliable material which can be used to build up the nose, or any other part of your face. It will not withstand much facial movement, and so should be used with care.

First wipe the skin completely free of grease. Knead the putty with a little petroleum jelly on your fingers to stop it sticking to them. If it is not sufficiently pliable, warm it or add a little cold cream.

It is possible to mould the putty straight on to your nose: press firmly to make it stick to your face and blend with your skin. If this does not work paint your nose with spirit gum and let it dry before applying the putty.

Smooth off the finished false nose with petroleum jelly to remove any cracks. Finally, powder before adding the make-up colour to blend in with your face.

To remove nose putty cut it away with a cotton thread used like a cheese wire.

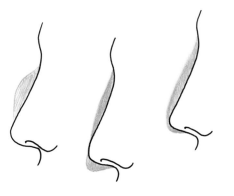

CREATING A DEEP SCAR

This is done with liquid latex.

Brush the latex on to the area to be scarred. Let it dry before squeezing it together to form a crease.

For a bloody scar paint it with blood and wipe it off.

BALD HEADS

Special rubber caps can be obtained from make-up manufacturers to fit over a head. They must be glued to the forehead with spirit gum before being carefully merged with the face by a make-up colour.

BEARDS AND MOUSTACHES

These are built up from crepe hair, sold in plaited hanks which must be unwound and straightened before use. Hold the hair over a steaming kettle to straighten it out. Always mix two colours together to get a realistic result. Comb them together or simply mix them a few strands at a time. The hair is glued into place with spirit gum.
Paint the area with spirit gum and let it become tacky.

Apply the crepe a few hairs at a time, starting at the base under the chin. Always use longer hairs than you need. The beard can always be trimmed after it is in place. Press the hair into place with your scissors and, when necessary, with a damp towel. Work upwards to the chin itself, continue on to the cheeks and finally add the moustache in two separate pieces.
Trim the beard to shape.

Glossary

A

Anti-pros (US) see Front-of-House lights

Apron extension of stage beyond the proscenium

ASM assistant stage manager

Auditorium area in which the audience is accommodated during the performance

B

Backcloth cloth usually painted, suspended from Flies at the rear of the stage

Backing (1) cloth or solid pieces placed behind doorways and other openings on sets to conceal stage machinery and building (2) financial support for a production

Bar horizontally flown rod (usually metal) from which scenery, lighting and other equipment are suspended

Bar bells bells sounded in all front-of-house areas to warn audience that the performance is about to continue. Operated from prompt corner, and so usually written into prompt copy

Barndoor adjustable shutters attached to stage lights to control the area of light covered by a particular lamp

Batten (1) see Bar (2) piece of wood attached to flown cloth to straighten it and keep it taut (3) piece of wood joining two flats (4) a group of stage lights suspended over the stage

Beam light a light with no lens, giving a parallel beam

Beginners call given by deputy stage manager to bring those actors who appear first in the play to the stage

Bifocal spot spotlight with additional shutters to allow hard and soft edges

Black light ultra violet light

Blocking the process of arranging moves to be made by the actor

Board lighting control panel

Book (1) alternative term for the scripts (2) the prompt copy (3) the part of a musical show conducted in dialogue

Book flat two flats hinged together on the vertical

Booking closing a book flat

Boom a vertical lighting bar

Boom arch used to hang a lantern from a boom

Border flown scenic piece designed to conceal the upper part of the stage and its machinery or equipment

Box set setting which encloses the acting area on three sides. Conventionally in imitation of a room in which the fourth wall has been removed

Brace portable support for flats

Bridge walkway above the stage used to reach stage equipment

C

Call (1) warning given at intervals to technicians and actors that they are needed on stage (2) notice of the time at which actors will be required to rehearse a particular scene

Callboard notice board on which calls and all other information relevant to the production should be posted

Cans headsets used for communication and co-ordination of technical departments during a performance

Centreline imaginary line drawn from rear to front of stage and dividing it exactly in half. Marked as CL on stage plans

Channel a circuit in the lighting or sound system

Chase a repeated sequence of changing lighting states

Check to diminish the intensity of light or sound on stage

Cinemoid a colour medium or filter

Circuit the means by which a lantern is connected to a dimmer or patch panel

Clamp C or G clamps are attached to lights to fasten them to bars

Cleat fixing on the back of flats to allow them to be laced together (cleated) with a sash line or cleat line. Also a metal fly rail to which ropes are tied

Clothscene scene played before downstage drop or tabs, while a major scene change takes place

Colour call the list of coloured gels required for a lighting design taken from the plan of the lighting design

Colour frame holder for the colour medium or filter in front of the light

Colour Medium translucent filter material placed in front of lights to give a coloured illumination

Colour wheel in lighting, a device attached to lamps which, when rotated, changes the colour medium through which the light is shown

Come down (1) instruction to actor to move towards the audience (2) instruction to lower intensity of sound or light (3) end of performance; time when curtain comes down

Corner plate triangle of plywood used to reinforce the corners of a flat

Counterweights mechanical system used for raising and lowering flown scenery

Counterweight flying the system of flying scenery, lights etc., whereby the flown item is balanced by counterweights

Crossfade the practice of moving to a new lighting or sound effect without intervening darkness or silence: one effect fades out simultaneously with the new one's being brought into play

Crossover (1) the device on a sound system that routes the sound of the correct pitch to the correct part of the loudspeaker; (2) the space behind the stage setting or below the stage through which actors can get from one side of the stage to the other without being seen by the audience

Cue (1) verbal or physical signal for an actor to enter or speak a line (2) point at which an effect is executed or business takes place

Cue light box with two lights, red and green, which warn an actor or technician to standby (red) and then do (green) whatever is required of them. Ensures greater precision when visibility or audibility is limited

Cue sheet list of particular effects executed by one department in a production

Cue-to-cue rehearsal of technical effects in a production with actors. The scene is rehearsed in sections beginning with a cue for standby, and concluding when the effect is finished

Curtain call process of actors appearing at the end of the play to receive audience applause. Formerly actors were called before the curtain by the audience

Curtain speech out of character address to the audience by a cast member or participant

Curtain up (1) time at which a play begins (2) a call given to the company to warn them the performance has begun

Cut cloth vertical scenic piece cut to reveal more scenery behind it. Most common in musicals

Cutting list list of materials required for scenery and set construction together with the correct dimensions of the pieces

Cyclorama undecorated backing to a stage, usually semi-circular and creating a sense of space and height. Often some theatres have permanent or standing cycloramas which have actually been built. The term is always abbreviated to cyc

D

Dead (1) the point at which a piece of scenery reaches the desired position onstage (2) a redundant production or scenic element

Decibel dB the measurement of volume of sound

Diffusion (colour) used like a gel but to soften and spread the beam of light rather than to colour it. Also called a frost

Dim the process of decreasing the intensity of light onstage

Dimmers the apparatus whereby lights are electrically dimmed

Dip small covered hole in stage floor with electric sockets

Dock area at side or rear of stage where scenery is stored when not in use

Downstage part of stage nearest to audience

Dress circle also known as the circle. Area of seating above the stalls and below the balcony

Dressing items used to decorate a setting

Dress parade the final check of costumes before the first dress rehearsal. The cast parade each of their costumes in order before the Director and Costume Designer so that any final alterations can be made

Drop suspended cloth flown into stage area

DSM deputy stage manager

Dutchman (US) thin piece of material used to cover the cracks between two flats

E

Elevation a working drawing usually drawn accurately and to scale, showing the side view of the set or lighting arrangement

Ellipsoidal the type of reflector used in many profile spots

Entrance (1) place on a set

through which the actor may appear (2) point in the script at which an actor appears

Exit (1) the process of leaving the stage (2) point in the script at which an actor leaves the stage

F

Fader a means of controlling the output level of a lantern (lamp) or amplifier

False proscenium construction placed behind the real theatre proscenium for decorative or practical purposes

Fit-up installation of lighting, technical equipment and scenery onstage when coming into a theatre

Flash-out system to check whether the lights are functioning properly by putting them on one at a time

Flat scenic unit comprised of wood or stretched cloth applied to a timber frame and supported so that it stands vertical to the stage door. Door flats and window flats have these openings in them. Masking flats are placed at the outer edges of the acting area to disguise areas of the stage from the public

Flies area above the stage in which scenery, lighting and other equipment are kept. If whole backdrops are to be stored then the flies should be at least twice the height of the stage opening

Floodlights also called floods. Lights which give a general fixed spread of light

Floorcloth painted canvas sheets placed on the stage floor to give a specific effect

Floor pocket (US) see dip

Flown (1) scenery or equipment which has been suspended above the stage (2) flown pieces are any scenic elements which will be made to appear or disappear from view in sight of the audience.

Fly the process of bringing scenery in and out of the stage area vertically

Flying (1) the process of stocking the flies (2) special effects whereby actors are suspended by wires to create the illusion of flying

Fly floor gallery at either side of the stage from which the flies are operated

Floats see footlights

Focusing the process of fixing the exact area to be lit by each light onstage

FOH Front-of-house. Any part of the theatre in front of the proscenium arch

Follow spot light directed at actor which can follow all movements

Footlights lights set into the stage at floor level which throw strong general light into performers' faces downstage

Fourth wall imaginary wall between audience and actors which completes the naturalistic room

French brace support for scenery fixed to stage

Fresnel type of spotlight with a fresnel lens which gives an even field of light with soft edges

Frontcloth see cloth

Front-of-House lights lights hung in front of the proscenium arch

Frost see diffusion

G

Gauze painted cloth screen, opaque when lit from the front, that becomes transparent when lit from behind. Often used at front of stage to diffuse total stage picture

Gel Colour medium introduced before light to alter colour of beam

Get-in/out (US) see fit-up process of bringing scenery into or taking it out of the theatre

Ghost a beam of light which inadvertently leaks from a light and falls where it is not wanted

Gobo (1) screen introduced before a stage light to give a particular image onstage (2) cut out shape that is projected

Green room general area in which cast and crew wait during performance

Grid metal frame from which all flying equipment is suspended

Groundrow raised section of scenery usually depicting bushes rocks etc.

Grouping (US) see blocking

H

Half half hour call. Warning to company given thirty-five minutes before performance

Handprop any prop handled by an actor, such as a handbag, walking stick, umbrella

Hanging attaching flying pieces to appropriate bars

Hook clamp the device that holds a lantern onto a bar

Hot lining the method by which lanterns, bulbs and cables are checked during rigging

House (1) audience (2) in opera, the entire theatre, and by implication, the company

I

Impedance a term for the electrical resistance found in a/c circuits, thus affecting the ability of a cable to transmit sound as electrical pulses. Measured in ohms

In one (US) see clothscene

Inset a small scene set inside a larger one

Iris a device within a lantern which allows a circular beam to be altered through a range of sizes

Iron a fire proof curtain that can be dropped downstage of the tabs in case of fire. Today it is usually made of solid metal and is electrically operated

K

Kill instruction to cease use of particular effect in lighting or sound

L

Ladder a ladder-shapped frame used for hanging side lights. It cannot usually be climbed

Lamp unit of lighting equipment

Lantern see lamp

Left stage left. That part of the stage to the actor's left when he is facing toward the audience

Leg cloth suspended vertically from flies and used to mask sides of stage and small areas within it

Levels (1) indicates intensity or volume of light or sound (2) raised areas onstage used for acting

Limes jargon for follow spots and their operators

Line drawings (US) see technical drawing

Linnebach projector used for projecting a picture from a gel or glass slide onto the set. Often used to give a shadow effect

Load in/out (US) see get in/out

Lose to turn off lighting or sound, or to remove an article from the set

Luminaire international term for lighting equipment. Not restricted to theatrical lighting

M

Marking (1) in use of props or scenery, the deployment of substitutes for the real object during rehearsal (2) in singing, a

means of using the voice with reduced volume and without vocalising extremes of register (3) any account of a role in which the full powers are not being used by the performer in order to save resources

Maroon a pyrotechnic giving the effect of a loud explosion

Mark out the system of lines and objects set on a rehearsal room floor to indicate the exact position of scenery and furniture. Marking out is the process of doing this

Mask to hide or conceal unwanted areas or machinery. Also used to describe one actor obscuring another unintentionally

MD musical director

Memory memory board. An advanced type of lighting control system where the required levels are stored electronically

Mezzanine area of seating above the orchestra and below the balcony. When a theatre has only a single balcony, first several rows are frequently designated the mezzanine

Mixer sound controls desk, used to mix and adjust levels of sounds from various sources

O

Offstage any backstage area not seen by the audience. Most specifically used to indicate the areas at the actor's right and left

OP opposite prompt. Stage Right (US Stage left)

Orchestra (US) see stalls

Out flying term for up

Overture (1) the music which begins a performance (2) a call to the actors and technicians that the performance is about to begin in a musical work

P

PA system the public address or any sound amplification system

Pack a number of flats all stored together

Pan (1) movement of lighting from side to side (2) used to describe water-based stage make-up (pancakes) (3) term (now nearly obsolete) to describe theatre sound installation

Parcan type of lantern which holds a par lamp

Patch border panel a panel at which the circuits governed by individual lighting dimmers can be changed

Perch lighting position concealed behind the proscenium

Periactus a tall, prism-shaped piece of painted scenery which can be revolved to show various phases

Pipe (US) see bar

Places please (US) see beginners

Platform (US) see rostrum

Plot (1) commonly used to describe the action of a play (2) any list of cues for effects used in the play

PM production manager

Practical any object which must do onstage the same job that it would do in life, or any working apparatus e.g. a light switch or water tap (faucet)

Preset (1) used to describe any article placed in its working area before the performance commences (2) also describes a basic lighting state that the audience sees before the action begins

Projector (US) see floodlight

Prompt copy fully annotated copy of the play with all the production details from which the show is run each time it is performed

Properties props. Any item or article used by the actors in performance other than costume and scenery

Props skip basket or cupboard in which props are kept when not in use

Props table table in convenient offstage area on which all properties are left prior to performance and to which they should be returned when dead

Pros proscenium arch the arch which stands between stage and auditorium. A pros arch theatre is a conventional theatre with a proscenium arch, usually without a forestage

PS prompt side. Conventionally meaning stage left, the term now refers only to the side of the stage in which the prompt corner will be found. In the US the PS is generally stage right

Prompt corner desk and console at the side of the stage from which the stage manager runs the show

Pyrotechnics any chemical effects used onstage or in wings to create lighting or special effects

Q

Quarter back stage pre-show call given twenty minutes before curtain up (ie. fifteen minutes before beginners)

R

Rail bottom or top batten of the frame of a flat

Rake the incline of a stage floor away from the horizontal; a raked stage is higher at the upstage end than at the downstage

Readthrough early rehearsal at which the play is read without action. Usually accompanied by discussion

Reflectors the shiny surfaces in the back of lighting equipment which help intensify the beam

Rigging the means of fixing lamps to appropriate bars before lighting a production

Right stage right. That part of the stage to the actor's right when he is facing the audience

Risers the vertical part of a stage step

Rostrum a raised platform sometimes with a collapsible frame used for giving local prominence to certain areas onstage

Run (1) the number of scheduled performances of a work (2) abbreviated form of run through

Runners a pair of curtains parting at the centre and moving horizontally

S

Saturation rig an arrangement of lights in which the maximum number of spotlights is placed in every possible position

Scatter the light outside the main beam of a spot

Scrim (US) see gauze

Seque musical term indicating that one number should go immediately into the next

Set to prepare the stage for action. To set up is to get ready. To set back is to return to the beginning of a given sequence

Shutter device in front of lamp to alter shape of beam

Single purchase counterweight flying system where the cradle travels the same distance as the fly bar's travel. The counterweight frame therefore occupies the full height of the side wall of the stage

Sightlines the angles of visibility from the auditorium

SM stage manager

Snap line chalk line, chalked piece of string which when stretched tight is used for making straight lines on stage

Special piece of lighting equipment whose main function is to perform a particular effect

Spiking see marking

Spill unwanted light onstage

Spot spotlight. Light giving a small circle of light, the dimensions of which can be precisely controlled by focusing

Stagger-run runthrough at which the production is pieced together, aiming at fluency but allowing for corrective stops

Stalls floor level area of seating in the auditorium

Strike instruction to remove any redundant or unnecessary object from stage

Super non-speaking actor not specifically named in the text

Swag curtains or tabs gathered together so they do not hang straight

Switchboard board from which lights are controlled

T

Tabs theatre curtains, most usually the House curtain

Tabtrack metal track on which the tabs run allowing them to open and close

Tallescope extendable ladder on wheels used in rigging and focusing lights and for minor corrections to flown pieces

Teaser short flown border used to mask scenery or equipment

Tech technical rehearsal at which all technical effects are rehearsed in the context of the whole production

Theatre in the Round acting area with audience on all sides

Throw in lighting, the distance between a light source and the object lit

Thrust stage type of stage which projects into the auditorium so that the audience can sit on at least three sides

Tilt the vertical movement of light

Tormentor (US) see teaser

Trap hole cut in stage and concealed by floor allowing access from below. Grave traps are usually double traps creating the illusion of a grave or pit. Once a common part of all theatres traps are now becoming increasingly rare

Trapeze single short hung lighting bar

Treads the flat part of stage steps

Truck movable cradle upon which scenery is placed to facilitate its movement

U

Upstage in a proscenium or thrust stage the area furthest away from the audience

W

Wagon (US) see truck

Walk-through rehearsals at which actors go through entrances, moves and exits to make clear any changes or alterations made necessary through change of cast or venue

Warning bells (US) see Bar bells

Ways the maximum number of combinations of channels on a lighting installation

Wings the sides of the stage concealed from the audience's view

Work-out in a dance or movement rehearsal, a vigorous session to prepare the body for specific work

Workshop any non-performing backstage area of a theatre

Workshop performance a performance in which maximum effort goes towards acting and interpretation rather than sets or costumes

Musical theatre special glossary

Andante walking space

Allegro happily, lightly

Allargando getting broader

Coda last section of music, often in a different tempo or mood

Cadence the resolving chords in music

Largo broadly

Lento slowly

Maestoso majestically

Presto fast

Aria solo, usually reflective in content

Duet musical number for two singers

Trio three singers

Quartet four singers

Ensemble (1) together (2) place in which all the characters all sing together

Finale (1) the end (2) by extension, a musical sequence which ends each act, often comprising different musical material but having an overall shape

MD musical director

Band parts the individual copies required by each player in an orchestra and containing only the notes for their particular instrument.

BIBLIOGRAPHY

Listed below are a
representative selection
of books for each of the
titles in this series.

In the United Kingdom Spotlight
publish annually *Contacts*, a complete guide to the British Stage,
TV, Screen and Radio (7 Leicester
Place, London WC2. Tel: 071 437
7631)

In the United States the Theatre
Communications Group Inc.
(TCG) (355 Lexington Avenue,
New York, NY 10017. Tel: 212
697 5230) has a publications
department which publishes not
only plays and books but also a
monthly magazine of news and
features called *American Theatre*.
It also publishes an employment
bulletin for the performing arts
called Art SEARCH.

Bentley, Eric *Theory of the Modern
Stage*, London, 1968

Brook, Peter *The Empty Space*,
London, 1985

Brown, John R *Drama and the
Theatre*, London, 1971

Hoggett, Chris *Stage and the
Theatre*, London, 1971

Oren Parker, Smith, W L, Harvey
R *Scene Design and Stage Lighting*,
London, 1979

Stanlislawski, K *An Actor Prepares*,
London, 1981

Costume and Make-up

Barton, Lucy *Historic Costume for
the Stage*, Boston, 1938

Barton, Lucy *Period Patterns*,
Boston, 1942

Corson, Richard *Fashions in Hair*,
London, 1985

Corson, Richard *Stage Make-up*,
New York 1960

Cunnington, Phillis and Lucas,
Catherine *Occupational Costume in
England*, London, 1967

Directing a Play

Berry, Cicely *Voice and the Actor*,
London and New York, 1974

Hagen, Uta and Frankel, Haskel
Respect for Acting, New York,
1980

Hodgson, John and Richards,
Ernest *Improvisation*, London,
1978; New York, 1979

Nicoll, A *The Development of the
Theatre*, London and New York,
1966

Willett, John *The Theatre of Bertolt
Brecht*, London, 1983; New York,
1968

Lighting and Sound

Bentham, Fredrick *Art of Stage
Lighting*, London, 1980; New
York, 1968

Burris-Meyer, H and Mallory, V
Sound in the Theatre, New York,
1979

Moore, J E *Design for Good
Acoustics*, London, 1961; New
York, 1979

Pilbrow, Richard *Stage Lighting* ,
London and New York, 1979

Reid, Francis *Stage Lighting
Handbook*, London, 1982; New
York, 1976

Stage Design and Properties

Govier, Jacquie *Create Your Own
Stage Props*, London and New
York, 1984

Leacroft, Richard and Helen
Theatre & Playhouse, London,
1984

Molinari, Cesare *Theatre Through
the Ages*, London and New York,
1975

Oren Parker, W L Smith, Harvey,
R *Scene Design and Stage Lighting*
London and New York, 1979

*Stage Management and Theatre
Administration*

Baker, Hendrik *Stage Management
and Theatre Craft, (3rd Edition)*,
London and New York, 1981

Bond, David *Stage Management:
A Gentle Art*, London 1991

Crampton, Esme *A Handbook of
the Theatre*, London and New
York, 1980

Gruver, Bert *The Stage Manager's
Handbook*, New York, 1972

Reid, Francis *The Staging
Handbook*, New York, 1978

SUPPLIERS
AND
STOCKISTS

Listed below are a representative selection of suppliers and
stockists.

UNITED KINGDOM

Costume, Props and Make-Up

Angels and Bermans
40 Camden Street
London NW1 0DX
Tel: 0171 387 0999
Fax: 0171 383 5603

Bapty and Co. Ltd (weapon hire)
703 Harrow Road
London NW10 5NY
Tel: 0181 969 6671
Fax: 0181 960 1106

Borovick Fabrics Ltd (theatrical)
16 Berwick Street
London W1V 3RG
Tel: 0171 437 2180/0520
Fax: 0171 494 4646

Bristol Old Vic Hire
Units 1 and 2
Hayward Road Industrial Estate
Staple Hill
Bristol BS16 4NT
Tel: 0117 970 1026

Brodie and Middleton (dyes,
canvas, metal powders and other
paints)
68 Drury Lane
London WC2B 5SP
Tel: 0171 836 3289
Fax: 0171 497 8425

Freed of London Ltd (theatrical shoes)
94 St Martin's Lane
London WC2N 4AS
Tel: 0171 240 0432
Fax: 0171 240 3061

Laurence Corner (period hats and other unusual clothing)
62 Hampstead Road
London NW1 2NU
Tel: 0171 813 1010
Fax: 0171 813 1413

Lighting and Sound

DHA Lighting Ltd
3 Jonathan Street
London SE11 5NH
Tel: 0171 582 3600
Fax: 0171 582 4779

Jim Laws Lighting
West End Lodge
Wrentham
Beccles
Suffolk NR34 7NH
Tel: 0502 675 264
Fax: 0502 675 565

MAC (Sound Hire)
1 and 2 Attenburys Park Road
Altrincham
Cheshire WA14 5QE
Tel: 0161 969 8311
Fax: 0161 962 9423

Northern Stage Services Ltd
Unit 1, Trent Industrial Estate
Duchess Street
Shaw
Oldham OL2 7UT
Tel: 0170 684 9469
Fax: 0170 684 0138

Strand Lighting
Grant Way
Isleworth
Middlesex TW7 5QD
Tel: 0181 560 3171
Fax: 0181 568 2103

Theatre Project Sound Services
13 Field Way
Bristol Road
Greenford
Middlesex UB6 8UN
Tel: 0181 813 1112
Fax: 0181 566 6365

White Light Electrics Ltd
57 Filmer Road
London SW6 7JF
Tel: 0171 731 3291
Fax: 0171 371 0806

Stage Equipment

British Harlequin
Kent House
High Street
Farningham DA4 0DT
Tel: 0132 286 5288
Fax: 0132 286 4803

CCT lighting
Hindle House
Traffic Street
Nottingham NG2 1NE
Tel: 0115 986 2722
Fax: 0115 986 2546

Flint Hire and Supply Ltd
35 Queen's Row
London SE17 2PX
Tel: 0171 703 9786
Fax: 0171 708 4189

Northern Light
39 Assembly Street
Leith
Edinburgh EH6 7RG
Tel: 0131 553 2383
Fax: 0131 553 3296

Northern Light
79 Loanbank Quadrant
Govan
Glasgow G51 3HZ
Tel: 0141 440 1771
Fax: 0141 445 4406

Rex Howard (Drapes) Ltd
Acton Park Industrial Estate
Eastman Road
The Vale
London W3 7QS
Tel: 0181 740 5881
Fax: 0181 740 5994

UNITED STATES

It is impossible to give a comprehensive list of suppliers and stockists in the space available. Those wishing to find a specific supplier should consult *Theatre Crafts Directory* (P.O. Box 470, Mt Morris, Illinois 61054 - 0470). This publication gives a comprehensive list of suppliers for costume fabric, electrical supplies, dance-wear, curtains and drapes, film equipment, and flameproofing. It even lists about 50 suppliers of feathers for theatrical costumes!

Costume, Props and Make-Up

Norcosto Inc.
3203 North Highway 100
Minneapolis
Minnesota 55422
Tel: 612 533 2791
Fax: 612 533 3718

Stagecraft Industries
5051 North Lagoon Avenue
Portland
Oregon 97217
Tel: 503 286 1600
Fax: 503 286 3345

Tobins Lake Studios
7030 Old US 23
Brighton
Michigan 48116
Tel: 810 229 6666
Fax: 810 229 0221

Wolf and Co.
4301 Bryan Street 309
Dallas
Texas 75204
Tel: 214 823 1880
Fax: 214 823 5659

Lighting and Sound

Electronics Diversified
1675 NW 216th Avenue
Hillsboro
Oregon 97124
Tel: 503 645 5533
Fax: 503 629 9877

Hub Electric Inc.
6207 Commercial Road
Crystal Lake
Illinois 60014
Tel: 708 530 6860
Fax: 815 455 1499

Showco Inc.
201 Regal Row
Dallas
Texas 75247
Tel: 214 819 3100/630 1188
Fax: 214 630 5867

Stage Equipment

Peter Albrecht Corporation
6250 Industrial Court
Greendale
Wisconsin 53129 - 2432
Tel: 414 421 6630
Fax: 414 421 9091

INDEX